THE
AUTHORITY
OF
LOVE

All rights reserved. No part of this publication may be reproduced, distributed, or transmitted in any form or by any means, including photocopying, recording, or other electronic or mechanical methods, without the prior written permission of the publisher, except in the case of brief quotations embodied in critical reviews and certain other noncommercial uses permitted by copyright law.

For permission requests, contact Greg Williams at greg@kentuckyfamily.org or address below.

All Scriptures in Preface are NASB. All Scriptures in the rest of the book are NIV unless otherwise noted.

ISBNs
Print or paperback ISBN: 978-1-7362393-2-2
Kindle ISBN: 978-1-7362393-0-8
eBook ISBN: 978-1-7362393-1-5

Disclaimer: All names in personal stories throughout this book are changed for purpose of anonymity.

Williams, Greg
324 Timothy Drive
Nicholasville, KY 40356
www.loveandlordship.com
The authority of love/ Greg Williams
1. Christian life. 2. Spirituality. 3. Relationship. 4. Marriage/family. 5. Title.

Ordering information:
Contact Greg at greg@kentuckyfamily.org or 859.229.6504 for bulk orders of quantity discounts. Includes any ministry or faith-based organization that would like to partner with us to sell books for 20% of net profits.

Printed in the United States of America.

First Edition — December 2020

"Just this week, week seven of the imposed coronavirus quarantine, I was asked by a fellow Christian leader, 'Other than the Bible, what book have you read during this extended period of isolation at home that has been most personally inspirational?'

My answer was, Love and Lordship's "The Authority of Love" by my friend, Greg Williams.

It is Biblical, clear, transparent and relevant:

- Books that are intended to be discipling tools, especially for men, must have the authority of God's Word laced into the text. Men will pay attention when God is allowed to speak. The exposition of scripture and the illustrations from scripture underpin the content of the book at every turn of a page.

- Greg is a linear thinker... like me! His book is logical. There is no way to get lost chasing 'rabbit trails' because there are none. He lays a foundation and then moves us step-by-step down a path of understanding the motives and methods for becoming a more devoted disciple of Jesus Christ.

- I am not sure I have ever read a book in which the author has been as open and honest as Greg. His humility in sharing his life journey is both endearing and engaging. Again and again he draws us into his story, a story with which the reader will easily identify.

- Greg is not an ivory-tower theologian. He is a down-to-earth practitioner of faithful Christian living. Love and Lordship is in touch with the real 'world, flesh and devil' and how each seeks to threaten and corrupt our daily walk with Christ.

[Don't start reading this book at 10:00 PM at night! You may find yourself groggy from lack of sleep the next day...]"

— Dr. Ken Idleman, Former President,
Ozark Christian College (1979 – 2006)
V.P. of Leadership Development for The Solomon Foundation

I am delighted to recommend Greg Williams' latest book "The Authority of Love." This book is grounded firmly in Biblical principles for marriage, family and the Christian home. These are timeless truths Greg has taught for many years. He not only teaches but models them in his own life, marriage and parenting. This book will be particularly helpful for discipleship and small group studies. When I pastored a local church Greg came and taught these principles. His lessons were very well received and desperately needed in a day when marriage, family and home are under attack."

— Wally Rendel, Senior Minister (Retired)
Jessamine Christian Church
Nicholasville, KY

My wife and I had the privilege of attending Greg's 7-session Love and Lordship event held at our church. Those sessions were extremely well done and everyone from our church loved them. I've since used some of his materials in my pre-marriage counseling sessions. Greg's passion for marriage and the family lights up the stage. We were so impressed with that first event that we had Greg come back and lead one of our churchwide group sessions as well. This book will be a great tool for those looking to fulfill God's covenant design for marriage and family."

— Terry Cooper, Senior Minister
Ninevah Christian Church
Lawrenceburg, KY

Section 4

Relationships: What We Were Created For

12. The Currency of Christ's Kingdom:
    Loving Relationships 67
13. Love & Lust...Pornography & Porneia 73
14. Self & Lust: A Modern Day Movie
    Biblical Story Mash-up 81
15. The Full-Orbed Love of God 85
16. God's Covenant Order 89
    Study Guide 93

Section 5

Marriage: In God's Image

17. Marriage is the #2 Priority 99
18. Building Agape Marriages & Kingdom Relationships 103
19. Biblical Tips for Navigating Marriage 109
20. Touching the Hot Topics 115
    Study Guide 118

Section 6

Marriage, Family & Parenting God's Way

21. Two Contrasting Stories of Home 125
22. God's Design for Parenting & Family 129
23. Character in Scripture 135
24. Biblical Discipleship in Parenting 139
25. Our Family Story: Discipling Our Children 143
    Study Guide 149

PREFACE

As I wrote this book, we found ourselves in the middle of the first global pandemic in a century as well as political and social upheaval in the USA like we've not seen in the last half-century. To say the least, we are in trying times and our faith is being tested. I believe God is calling Christ's Church to a spiritual awakening.

That awakening is not just simply to do church services differently, serve more people and accommodate the culture thinking we will reach more. It is a call...

- For personal and collective confession and repentance of idolatry and compromise;
- For believers to absolutely make Christ Lord of every part of your life;
- For men to be Godly relational servant leaders, as husbands who love their marriage, spouse and family above their own success, glory and desires, just as Christ did for His Bride, The Church;
- For marriages to be a positive testimony to the Gospel of Christ so the world will see and know Him;
- To husbands and wives to submit to one another out of reverence for and submission to Christ as Lord;
- To disciple our children in our homes and, in all of the above, to build loving relationships that strengthen Christ's Church;
- To move beyond drawing people into a weekly one-hour service or a couple hours of weekly activity to our communities or the world;
- To disciples making disciples in loving relationships and holding each other accountable to obedience as we walk in His Love and Lordship;

That call is the message of this book.

Regarding the credit for this book, I must first acknowledge Jesus Christ, my Savior and Lord. Without His Truth and grace in love not only would this book be impossible but my life would be a mess. Thank You, Jesus, over and over again!

I must also thank my beautiful and wonderful wife, and editor of this book, Ami. She is the light of my earthly life as we have walked this journey together in Christ. "An excellent wife, who can find? For her worth is far above jewels. The heart of her husband trusts in her, and he will have no lack of gain. She does him good and not evil all the days of encouragement by several great friends (see above), opportunity, and timing, as well as the preparation of my heart and mind over the years comes at this time.

I began writing just after the celebration of my parents' 60th anniversary. Elliott and Peggy Williams, I love you and congratulations on a rare milestone that very few reach and an incredible testimony to God's faithful commitment in covenant love! Thank you for your example to me and my family and so many others! Coincidence? I don't think so, and you'll see why throughout this book.

Far too often, nearly every single man and couple that I counsel, mentor, or speak with comes from a church background (past and present) and has very little idea what Christ's Love and Lordship means according to His Word. They attend church and often are in a small group. Their children attend children's and youth ministry and they sign up and serve, but their understanding of God's Word is lacking at best and usually nearly absent—and it is very evident in their marriage and family.

This is a wakeup call to the modern-day American church (and wherever it has been exported) to place the priorities of discipleship in loving relationships—beginning with marriage and family in the home—above attendance, conversions, and success.

It cannot be just an occasional teaching on marriage as one man/one woman for life, but prioritizing it in everything that is done. It's teaching, building, and holding accountable young people and all people (those unmarried, married, and divorced) to the high standards of God's Word in relational and sexual purity and integrity. It is encouraging ALL to honor marriage (Hebrews 13:4) and to seek and extend the high calling of relational servant-leadership in Christ's Church to those who have lived accordingly (1 Timothy 3:4-5).

Love & Lordship, from which this book springs, is a ministry and message that calls those who claim Christ as Savior and Lord to display the image of God in these four areas in their life and relationships:

1) Christ as Lord in all things reflected in...

2) Loving Marriages/Families/Relationships that lead to...

3) Relational Servant-leadership first in marriages and families and develops...

4) Generational Discipleship in personal life, life, family, The Church, and culture.

We want to encourage and challenge those who will take this to heart to allow it to drive them to Christ, His Spirit, and His Word, and into a relationship with Him as Lord and relationships with all others that reflect His Love.

INTRODUCTION

This is not politically correct, but I need to say it: if you're not serious about walking with Christ as your Lord and you as His disciple, building deep loving relationships in Him—especially marriage and family—doing so for the sake of His Church and Kingdom, this book is likely not for you. If you are serious, then read on!

"But make sure that in your hearts you honor (set apart) Christ as Lord. Always be ready to give an answer to anyone who asks you about the hope you have. Be ready to give the reason for it. But do it gently and with respect." (1 Peter 3:15 / NIRV) (parentheses mine and added)

I grew up in a very church going (every time the doors were open) Christian family as an "all-American" kid. I got good grades, played the piano, sang in choir, played sports, and was sheltered from much of the world. My life consisted of church, family, school, farm, and basketball—not necessarily in that order.

Ah, church! Well that was just as much a success pursuit as anything else. Early on in Sunday School class or Christian service camps, we'd get a gold star for attendance, extra points for the number of Bible chapters read, and even more points for Bible verses memorized. While I loved the little prizes we'd get and competitions we'd win for these spiritual endeavors, the best part was the recognition it would bring. Everyone "oohed and aahed" whenever I would tell how many chapters I read and how many verses I memorized. And with all those points my team could win! That was awesome!

It all looked and sounded good, but it was rooted in my pride and flesh. You don't tell a hyper-competitive boy or young man that he can win by reading and memorizing the Bible and doing the most service projects. I worked hard to accomplish the next challenge, always for The Lord and His Church, of course. Every win led to more prideful church service or volunteering in the community, which made the church—and me—look really good!

I spent much of college and a few years beyond thinking I knew more than God and pursued the athletic lifestyle. I chose to do relationships and sexuality my own way and as long as I went to church with my girlfriend(s) and treated them nicely then surely God was okay with it. Partying was fine because everyone else was doing it. The enemy and world were all too willing to accommodate as I kept up the façade of the nice, "all-American," Christian young man.

Whenever I stepped outside my own ever-expanding boundaries and felt a bit guilty I would simply show up at church, quote Scripture, have some spiritual conversations, worship, and enjoy a nice message—although occasionally the message would hit way too close to home for what I was experiencing. With my guilt assuaged I would walk a little straighter line

renewed insight and power. Every bit of this book comes from His Word by His Spirit in Christ's Authority.

As I spent time in His Word and presence, He began to shift my thinking from professional basketball to pouring into young people (in particular boys and young men) and continued to prune and shape me. Once again I "heard" God say to me, "I need someone to help raise up Godly men, marriages, and families because the enemy is wreaking havoc in these relationships and crippling My Church!"

So, right at the doorstep of realizing my dream of professional basketball player, The Lord clearly guided me to help raise up Godly men, husbands, and fathers—disciples of Christ.

I spent the next 14 years in teaching, coaching, and administration in public and private schools. I then shifted for the next eight years into directing a non-profit Sexual Risk Avoidance program and then transitioned into building the Kentucky Marriage Movement with The Family Foundation over the last nine years.

I had a mentor tell me that God has given me a story and by His grace I've won, as my mentor said, at marriage and family and that is why God has called me to speak to it. You will hear numerous stories and anecdotes throughout this book about our marriage and family as well as others that I've had the privilege to encourage, challenge and point to His Love and Lordship. Christ has saved us and given us His Holy Spirit so that we could be His witnesses to others (Acts 1:8).

As my mentor encouraged me to do, this story was a pivotal moment where I died to myself for the sake of my wife, marriage, and family, ultimately to honor Christ. That is what each of us must do in discipleship and in our marriages and families. Not necessarily the same decision but He must take priority and in order to do that, by His grace we must choose to decrease (John 3:30). That's how we become His witness...a testimony to His life in and through us!

During the early years of our marriage I was a high school athletic director and basketball coach. As I ended my time at one school and went to my second school as a head coach, I stepped into a team that was picked dead last in their region and predicted to go 3-25 that first year. We won 12 games that first year and 16 in the second year, finishing third in our region. We were slated to be first in the region the next year with eight of our top nine players returning.

As we neared the end of that second season and school year Ami found out she was pregnant with our third child that would be our precious Princess, Haidyn.

I knew that moving away from family and friends for this coaching job had been difficult for Ami as she knew no one and was raising two toddler boys. They were very good, but they were both "all boys." She had been a great support for me.

and marriages, and faithful husbands, fathers and families.

Through the years of learning and growing, God has shaped and pruned me, and this message for His Kingdom purpose, and He continues to confirm the calling.

You'll read how Ami and I started a young couples' class with another couple that grew from four to over 100 in just six months...

How two conversations, 19 years apart, with two pastors from two different continents clarified the formation and continuing of this message and ministry...

There are stories of men, women, marriages, and families whose lives have been radically changed by the Love and Lordship of Christ.

My hope and prayer is that your knowledge of the Bible and personal relationship with Jesus will grow exponentially after reading this book.

they've even chosen to walk the path of marriage). Love is lived out as feelings and emotions and when they get out of control, there is little love and a lot of accusations, demands and "lording it over" the little woman or manipulating the husband to get what he or she wants.

So, what is Love and Authority? God, in His Word, has much to say about authority and love and both are necessary to build Godly relationships that reflect His image and glory.

With that said, I want to make sure we're all speaking the same language and on the same page as you make your way through this book.

I don't know about you but I probably should have paid a bit more attention in English class (sorry Ms. Lake and Dr. Harrison) but in language there is a strong need to recognize and understand "root words." The root word found in any word gives us insight as to its meaning. If we don't know the root word, then we are either already lost and/or easily deceived.

Authority & The Author

As we focus on authority, we will see that in God's Kingdom Love and Lordship can never be separated.

Everybody knows that lordship is authority or control and love is a feeling, right? Unfortunately, these fallacies persist in our culture. Maybe that's the problem and why we need to better understand Authority.

As a matter of fact, that's exactly why we need to define key terms so readers understand what is being said according to the ***author***. Isn't that interesting—according to the author? Why do I embolden and italicize that word?

What do you think of when you hear "authority?"

When I'm sharing this message, in particular in prisons and addiction rehab facilities, the first answer is almost always, "Police," followed by "Courts, government," and "boss, manager, and superior." You get the picture.

When we come across the word "authority," many of us immediately think in terms of control, supervision, management, or ruling and lording over others. While authority may connote these ideas to some degree, we need to begin with the root word to truly understand what authority is.

So why italicize "author" earlier? Author is the root word of "authority." This means that before we define authority as controlling or ruling over someone by position or rank, we need to understand who the "author" is for that rank, position, or title.

In its simplest form, authority means pertaining to, or of, the author.

With this in mind, it would be wise of us to find out who is the author. Once we know who the Author is, we can determine what the Author meant by what was said or done. And we will know who is in authority.

I pray this book is convicting! If we are convicted that we are living according to God's plan and Word, then we will be encouraged to stand strong and keep the faith, individually and collectively. If, however, we are not following His plan and Word, and culture would seem to reveal there is much more "fruit" to indicate this to be the case, then our conviction will challenge us to humbly accept and change what we are doing for our sake, and even more importantly, for the sake of His Family and Kingdom.

By the way, here are Scriptures regarding God's Authority placed in Christ...

In **Matthew 28:18** Jesus said, "All authority has been given to me."
By whom? The answer is: God the Father gave it to him. Keep reading...

Matthew 11:27 "All things have been handed over to me by my Father, and no one knows the Son except the Father, and no one knows the Father except the Son and anyone to whom the Son chooses to reveal him."

John 3:35 "The Father loves the Son and has given all things into his hand."

John 13:3, 5 "Jesus, knowing that the Father had given all things into his hands, and that he had come from God and was going back to God...began to wash the apostles' feet."

Ephesians 1:20–21 "God raised him from the dead and seated him at his right hand in the heavenly places, far above all rule and authority and power and dominion, and every name that is named, not only in this age but also in the one to come."

John 17:2 "Father, the hour has come; glorify your Son that the Son may glorify you, for you granted him authority over all flesh, to give eternal life to all whom you have given him.

Philippians 2:9-11 "Therefore God exalted him to the highest place and gave him the name that is above every name that at the name of Jesus every knee should bow, in heaven and on earth and under the earth, and every tongue acknowledge that Jesus Christ is Lord, to the glory of God the Father."

Authority is Lordship & Leadership?

As stated earlier, authority, lordship and leadership are synonymous in line with their application in Scripture. God has some very specific things to say about authority and lordship, but unfortunately we tend to overlook, ignore, or redefine it with what works best for us in the moment. In so doing, we are almost always upside-down and missing what True Authority looks like and how we are to model and honor it.

The first and greatest command speaks to God's Authority, but it is often overlooked because "love," at least in our worldly definition, is so much more pleasant to talk about and live out. Look at what Jesus had to say when He was asked which was the most important command.

Mark 12:29-31 begins with, **"The most important one," answered Jesus, "is this: 'Hear, O Israel: The Lord our God, the Lord is one.** Love the Lord your God with all your heart and with all your soul and with all your mind and with all your strength.' The second is this: 'Love your neighbor as yourself.' There is no commandment greater than these." (Bold emphasis mine and added)

Before Jesus talks about love and its importance, He echoes what God told Moses in Deuteronomy 6:4-5. He states that God is alone, The One and Only, worthy of all our praise and worship. Every person hearing Moses, and Jesus, say these words would have understood that the priority command begins with recognizing and honoring God as Lord, as The Author, The One with All Authority. Everything else flows from this first and most important command.

Jesus clearly reinforced this before He left earth the first time in what we refer to as the Great Commission found in Matthew 28:18: "Then Jesus came to them and said, 'All authority in heaven and on earth has been given to me.'"

If we do not understand and accept that God is The One True Authority then nothing else lines up. We can define love and everything else the way we want. We can call the shots and be in control or at least have the appearance of being in control. And that's exactly what we do when we ignore The Author and His Truth.

Beginning with the Author impacts how we love, build relationships—especially marriage and family—and how we grow His Church and advance His Kingdom to influence the world and culture.

In order to have real leadership (authority), we should begin where God's Word begins: All Authority begins and ends with Christ. We seek leadership in our communities, state, and nation, in our businesses, schools, media, and churches. Yet Scripture outlines and teaches only two places where authority—headship or leadership—is to be developed: the Home (Ephesians 5:21-33) and the Church (Christ's Family), and leadership is to follow that order (1 Timothy 3:4-5).

Far too often we see so-called 'leaders' (those who wield the sword

"For by the grace given me I say to every one of you: Do not think of yourself more highly than you ought, but rather think of yourself with sober judgment, in accordance with the faith God has distributed to each of you." (Romans 12:3)

"For we are God's handiwork, created in Christ Jesus to do good works, which God prepared in advance for us to do." (Ephesians 2:10)

Knowing who we are in Christ is at the heart of understanding True Authority. He modeled it in His own life and asks us, by faith, to do the same. Knowing who we are recreated (He changes us or makes us new) to be in Him allows us to serve without consideration for what others think, or how the world ranks or rates us. We simply serve out of love and humility, confident and content in who we are so we can raise others above ourselves as we serve them. This is the essence of True Authority!

Modeling True Authority

"When he had finished washing their feet, he put on his clothes and returned to his place. "Do you understand what I have done for you?" he asked them. "You call me 'Teacher' and 'Lord,' (TRUE AUTHORITY) and rightly so, for that is what I am. Now that I, your Lord and Teacher, have washed your feet, you also should wash one another's feet. I have set you an example that you should do as I have done for you. Very truly I tell you, no servant is greater than his master, nor is a messenger greater than the one who sent him. Now that you know these things, you will be blessed if you do them." (John 13:12-17) (parentheses added and mine)

Jesus not only taught us what True Authority was, He modeled it! And then, He stated very clearly that if we want to have any authority in our lives it is to be exercised through our humble loving and serving of others. This is how True Authority is modeled and how we are blessed as we follow His example.

1) Godly character and integrity;
2) Able to teach and shepherd others;
3) Servant-leader (manager) in the marriage and family (absence of this clearly negates leadership in His Church);
4) Humble maturity in the faith and;
5) Have a good reputation in the community.

God is showing us True Authority and the priority of relationships from which it is to be learned, modeled, and lived out. In the relationships of marriage and family, character is developed, wisdom is honed, the humility that comes from wisdom (James 3:13) is derived, and evidently where every other area of leadership is to come from, including and especially in His Church. When we miss it in our homes, then we will struggle to find it in Christ's Church or anywhere else according to The Author.

True Authority in The World

"Jabez was more honorable than his brothers... Jabez cried out to the God of Israel, 'Oh, that you would bless me and enlarge my territory! Let your hand be with me, and keep me from harm so that I will be free from pain.' And God granted his request." (1 Chronicles 4:9a-10)

Known as the "Prayer of Jabez" this granted request carries a great deal of insight, not the least of which is the simple fact that Jabez's honor (character) was instrumental to God's granting the "enlargement of his territory," literally "greater influence." Character and servant-leadership (True Authority) go hand in hand in Scripture and yet there is a conspicuous absence of defining any 'leaders' in Scripture except for in the Home and Church. God wanted us to learn how to truly lead (serve) in the settings and relationships where the most is at stake.

John Adams, Founding Father and the second U.S. President stated, "Public virtue cannot exist in a nation without private, and public virtue is the only foundation of republics." For far too long we have sought our leaders in our state and nation and even churches (public virtue) from those who've simply had success in the corporate, financial, or other related realms. Often this was at the sacrifice of the personal life, the home, marriage, and family (private virtue), the very place where real relational servant-leadership is to begin, be learned and mature. Maybe we should heed God's Word and seek our Leaders from our marriages, families, homes, and from Christ's Church!

The Rest of The Story

I asked Dennis how loving and leading the way he'd always heard and seen it had worked for him? I asked him how well it was working now?

STUDY GUIDE
AUTHORITY & LOVE

Key Concepts

1) True Authority comes from The Author.
2) The world/culture defines and practices authority as control or lording over others.
3) God, The Author, defines/models in Christ, relational servant-leadership as authority.
4) Authority as relational servant-leadership begins in the marriage and family.
5) Authority in Christ's Church is to be an extension of good leadership in the home.
6) The world's authority prioritizes production, results, and success over people.
7) True Authority prioritizes people and relationships over things, outcomes, and success.

Discussion Questions

1) How have you seen authority practiced or modeled in your life, family, church or vocation?
2) How have you practiced authority in your life and relationships?
3) What do you think motivates us to practice authority as Gentiles, unbelievers or sinners?
4) What steps will you identify and take to practice authority as Christ taught and modeled it?
5) The last quote in this chapter by Oswald Chambers – how does that make you think differently about Christ's love and lordship and how you are to follow Him?
6) Would your home be different if you modeled relational servant-leadership?
7) How might your church be different? Your workplace?

hard, especially the ones that bring us the most and immediate reward. Sexual sin is one of the easiest to fall into and by far the most difficult to conquer and be freed from.

He knew The Lord but had decided, like so many others, that he was doing fine as he continued to live as he desired, show up at church, give a little money, and convince himself that all was well. After all, the reason we had connected was because he was dating a lady that went to our church and that was going pretty well.

About four months into our weekly discipleship we found ourselves in a deep conversation about lust, pornography, and sexual sin. He abruptly got up from the table at our usual restaurant meeting place and told me he'd explain the next week in person. He didn't want to share it over phone or email.

I wished him well and prayed for him as he hurried out the door. The following Thursday he came bounding into the restaurant with a big smile on his face and plopped down in our booth. He proceeded to tell me why he had so quickly left the week before, a story you'll read later in this section.

John was living much the same way as many others in our day and culture. Even if they attend church, it's usually not so much to know Jesus but to interact and mingle, assuage their conscience, and/or keep up appearances. Or maybe it's because their girlfriend, boyfriend or spouse, even their extramarital "partner" goes to church and that's their motivation. However, their lives do not reflect that Christ is Lord. They may be at church, but they are still looking in all the wrong places because their hearts do not fully belong to Him.

The fictitious Father Smith sums up how many live their lives apart from God unknowingly seeking Him, "The man who rings the bell at the brothel, unconsciously does so seeking God." (Bruce Marshall, *The World, The Flesh and Father Smith.*)

We could substitute various options for "brothel," and many of them are nice compromises that we've justified and condoned in place of Christ as Lord. We fill the emptiness with drugs, drink, food, sex, marriage, spouse, children, family, on and on—even "church." Many of these only destroy lives and several are very noble and worthy, but none should supersede Christ in our lives.

Augustine said it this way: "Thou hast made us for thyself, O Lord, and our heart is restless until it finds its rest in thee."

Christ as Lord

In Section 1 we discussed and determined that God as Father, Son, and Holy Spirit is the Authority and as such we need to look to Him, in particular to Christ, as The Father has placed all Authority in His hands.

I then follow up with this statement that sums up the initial step toward a solution to every person's or couples' problems: "All of the issues we will discuss today stem from the first two, but so often we only deal with the symptoms that occur in the latter two."

Lordship is of Utmost Importance

For some, the root issues become apparent right away. Yet often, as with John in our story above, we have to dig deeper to find what is really being fed or protected before the person will truly admit that they are trying to run their own life. As we will see, the enemy's greatest deception is, "You can be captain of your own ship, master of your own fate; you don't need a lord." He's simply appealing to our natural desire to be in authority, in control.

At this point I will ask the question, "How's that been working for you?"

Usually the light begins to flicker and maybe even come on. Now we can talk about why it is of utmost importance that Christ is Lord of our lives and the evidence, no matter how much we want to think otherwise, is that we have not made Him so.

Another of Satan's greatest deceptions is that in luring us away from The Author he can now get us to define words and concepts according to our whims and desires rather than according to God's Truth. We'll unpack the story of sin and the fall a bit later in this section to show you how the enemy lures and deceives us.

We alluded to this in Chapter 1, but we must take it further. I'm going to do so with perhaps the most misused and misunderstood word in all of language, especially in today's culture.

Dr. Gary Chapman, author of **Five Love Languages**, states, "Love is the most important word in the English language — and the most confusing."

I agree that it is the most confusing word, generally because we have defined it outside of God's Word and Authority as feelings or emotion-based and that is dangerous (see chart in next chapter). I don't agree that it is the most important word in our language, but the fact that we so often attribute it as such creates much confusion and many problems. We have chosen to relatively redefine terms, again falling for Satan's deception to lure us from God's Authority and Truth.

When I ask couples or conference attendees to define "love," we have nearly as many definitions as we do people. Why is that? Because we've fallen for the lie that "love" is whatever we want it to be in making us feel good and fulfilled. It's all rooted in feelings and satisfaction in the moment.

Paraphrasing NASA, "Church, we have a problem!"

No one argues or questions the worldly definitions; we've all lived them. Remember, "for all have sinned and fall short of the glory of God" (Romans 3:23). This is the root of the deception and sin.

As we apply Scripture defining each "TRUTH" along with the contrasting worldly concepts, we lay the foundation that helps us determine who is truly our lord/Lord and the impact that has on our lives. Following are the Scriptures and brief explanations that, again, help us grasp His Truth and whether or not we are walking with Him as Lord on this foundation.

1) Love as Commitment – The Truth lies in Christ and The Cross as the greatest example of Love ever given. In Matthew 26:53, "Do you think I cannot call on my Father, and he will at once put at my disposal more than twelve legions of angels?" With this statement, Jesus tells us He had a choice in the matter and that none of it felt good.

   Think about how Jesus felt relationally as His best friends all abandonedHim. (Matthew 26:56)

   How do you think He felt socially with the crowds crying, "Crucify Him!"? (Matthew 27:22-23)

   What about mentally and emotionally as He was in so much anguish in the garden that He sweat drops of blood? (Luke 22:44)

   Obviously He did not feel good physically as He was mocked, spit on, flogged, beaten, and crucified. (Matthew 26:67-68; 27; 26-31; Luke 23:33-34; John 19:1-17)

   One final thought on love and feelings: How do you think He felt spiritually as He cried out, "My God, My God, why have you forsaken me?" (Mark 15:34)

   Think about it, if love were a feeling, as our culture predominantly defines and lives it today in nearly every situation, then what would Jesus have done? He would have looked to His Father and said, "Nope, this feels awful and if 'love' is a feeling, this must not be love at all. I'm outta here!"

   Instead because God in Christ is the Author and Authority, the Truth is that love is a commitment. He loved His Father and us, so He remained committed and obedient (in love) to His Father and for us to show us what love truly is. "Father, forgive them For they do not know what they are doing." (Luke 23:34)

   By the way, we must understand that Jesus here is modeling the greatest commands for us. In Luke 22:42, we see Him petitioning the Father and fulfilling the greatest command by submitting to His Authority (Deuteronomy 6:4; Mark 12:29), asking if He could be spared from the cup of suffering and sacrifice if there was any other way. Obviously, the answer was no (a great lesson for all of us in that God always answers our prayers but not always as we

or undivided. If you remember your second grade math lessons, you'll know that an integer is a "whole number." Integrity is also found in the Hebrew word, "Shalom" which is most often interpreted as "peace." So what do whole numbers have to do with peace and integrity? I'm glad you asked.

Shalom, in Hebrew, actually has at least 27 related meanings, as we understand it in English. The closest English word to capturing the full meaning of Shalom is "completeness" or "wholeness."

Integrity or akeraiótita, from the same root word as integer or whole number, means much more than just making everything look good. It literally means uprightness and is found in wholeness. We find Shalom or peace when we apply the whole of God's Truth to every part of our lives. This is the character of integrity, not the world's compromise of reputation sufficing for character. I hope this brief explanation of terms has helped you. Even more so, it would serve you well to remember them in light of God's Truth as we dive deeper and apply them to every aspect of our lives and discipleship walk and relationships, especially in marriage, family, and His Church.

5) Finally, we come to discipleship. This is crucial in understanding Lordship as it defines our response to whoever is Lord/lord in our life. Just as profound, if not more so, is our understanding of the enemy's use of this in our lives. We will build on discipleship in Section Three.

time to know His Truth or can the enemy confuse you with the same question? 2) Note how cunningly Satan asked if God had restricted them from eating from any of the trees. He didn't just focus on the one God had forbidden as he wanted Eve to think it through to see if she truly knew the Truth of what God had said. How easily we can be deceived if we do not spend time in His Word to seek and know His Truth.

"We may eat of the fruit of the trees of the garden: But of the fruit of the tree which is in the midst of the garden, God hath said, You shall not eat of it, neither shall you touch it, lest you die." (vv. 2-3 NKJV) – Eve's reply reveals she had some knowledge of God's Absolute Truth, but it was incomplete. The question itself coupled with her partial knowledge accomplished two things that the serpent desired: 1) Partial truth led to her confusion and; 2) Her response literally "created" an alternate or relative "truth," one that likely worked in her favor. Now we have "two truths," God's (don't eat) and Eve's (don't touch). What to do? Relativism is not a modern or post-modern phenomenon; it is as old as human nature itself and the enemy used that very human nature and the free will necessary for love to exist to confuse and deceive. God's Absolute Truth can never be compromised. Don't fall for the lies.

"And the serpent said unto the woman, you shall not surely die." (v. 4 NKJV) – The serpent calls God a liar without even using His Name. He simply appeals to Eve's desire to live and recants God's Words, yet Eve still has not given in. The serpent is just laying the groundwork for his grand finale and the source of every sin since, including yours and mine.

"For God knows that when you eat from it your eyes will be opened, and **you will be like God, knowing good and evil.**" (v. 5, bold emphasis mine and added) – Ah, the coup de grace for the serpent (likely Satan but never stated in Genesis) that continues to appeal to every human being that has ever existed. And, according to Romans 3:23, all of us have fallen for it!

Deception & Relativism – Consent Replaces Covenant

I present the Love & Lordship series multiple times annually at prisons, residential addiction rehab facilities, and to other men's groups where many of them are ordered to attend by the court or government. After the first couple of sessions on Lordship and Discipleship, we dive into relationships, as seen in later sections.

When I get to the discussion on lust and porneia I often refer back to the original deception of Eve in the Garden by the serpent and equate it to how we redefine sexuality and sex to accommodate our own desires. I discuss how we create our own convenient "truths" to support what we want, whether that's stealing a piece of bubble gum when we're five years old (not that I ever did that) or anything else and justifying that it's perfectly fine if we didn't get caught. I ask the men if they have ever stolen anything and for years 100% of the hands went up.

On one particular day, three guys said they had not taken or stolen anything. I asked if they had ever taken any girl's virginity or virtue and they all said, "Oh, yeah." Immediately two of them then said, "But they willingly gave it (consented)."

The Holy Spirit immediately laid this on my heart: "Oh, so you consented and she consented, but God never consented. His Truth didn't change."

You could hear a pin drop! Isn't that how we choose the tree of knowledge of good and evil? We justify and rationalize our own truth for our own pleasure. We ignore His Truth when it doesn't fit what we want, but we will still have to answer to His Word and will.

Consent (our "truth") is a bad substitute for covenant and commitment (God's Truth). This is an example of falling for satan's lie that we can "be like God" and have our own kingdom that ultimately destroys many lives.

Path to Sin & The Fall

For practical purposes, check out the path below found in the serpent's temptation that led to Sin and The Fall of Adam and Eve and persists in our sins today. Think about how this applies to your life, temptations, sins, and struggles. Christ has made a way to rescue and redeem us.

1. Confusion – "Did God really say...?" Do I know His Truth?
2. Deception – "Surely you won't die." Do I fall for subtle lies?
3. Touch – "You must not touch it." Relativism leads to initial appeal to the flesh.
4. Taste – "Pleasing to the eye and desirable for gaining wisdom." Satisfy the flesh (senses and emotions rule rather than God's Truth).
5. Indulge – "She took some and ate it ... and he ate it." Please the senses (self).
6. Addiction/Bondage – "They realized they were naked... made coverings for themselves." Now caught in their sin they must cover it up.

Choosing to be obedient to Christ as His Lord, John and his girlfriend chose to remain abstinent until they were married six months later. He called me from their honeymoon to thank me and confirm that the sexual union of love in covenant was far better than any other that he had ever experienced.

Just like John, we all have the fruit(s) or temptations rooted in our selfish fleshly desires that we either know are wrong and pursue them anyway, or justify and deceive ourselves in pursuit of them. Their end is destruction as John found out. As he understood and began to walk with Jesus as Lord, everything changed.

Nearly 12 years later, John and his wife are now mentoring other couples to walk in The Lord.

What a beautiful blessing and reward to know your Lord! It will change everything for your good and His Glory. It's Discipleship and it's the only response that makes our lives worthwhile. Let's look further to find out what that entails.

STUDY GUIDE
THE LORDSHIP OF CHRIST

Key Concepts

1) Whoever is your Lord/lord or authority defines your Truth/truth.
2) There are only two Kingdoms and therefore two Kings (Lords).
3) Truth is Absolute and the Foundation for all things.
4) Lordship is based on Absolute Truth and is inherent in all of life/relationships.
5) Your choices reveal the priorities in your life.
6) Priorities reflect who/what is in control (Lord/lord) of your life.
7) All sin in life come from rebellion against His Lordship and failure to recognize and live in His Truth.
8) Christ's example shows us that authority is invited influence rather than demanding, manipulating, or controlling.
9) Humility and Integrity are essential in healthy lives and relationships.

Discussion Questions

1) Who/What is Lord in your life? What are your priorities?
2) How has 'Absolute Truth' been evident in your life?
3) Does Christ's example on the Cross change how you perceive and will apply love in your life and relationships?
4) What decisions have you rationalized and acted on apart from His Truth?
5) How has that played out in your life?
6) "In the world, authority is demanded, manipulated, and all about control and 'lording it over' others, even when we do it nicely. In God's Kingdom, authority is "invited influence in the lives of those who have willingly surrendered." How does this statement change or impact your view and application of authority?
7) What did you learn about 'Humilty' and how might that help you?
8) What did you learn about 'Integrity' and how might that help you?
9) Who are you a disciple of?

If Jesus Christ is King of kings and Lord of lords and He is. If Jesus Christ came to save all who believe in Him so we could be in a relationship with Him and He did. If you have received Him as Savior and claim to be in that relationship with Him, the only question that remains... are you submitting to Him as Lord of your life?

first 4-5 years. In time the guilt became too heavy and he confessed the porn to her. She practically cut him off from sex over the next four years. Though he tried to fight the temptation, he continued with porn and about three years after the confession he had an affair.

I shared with him that this was God's design coming true in the flesh: where the eyes and mind go the body will eventually follow.

She left him, and here he was sitting in my office having finally sought counsel as she had asked him to do years earlier after the initial porn confession. In pride, he had chosen not to do so.

He was heartbroken, full of guilt and shame, and missing his wife. She had made no contact with him for the four months following her departure.

He came into my office one week and said he was considering not continuing with any counseling or mentoring as it was doing no good. I asked what that meant and he said, "She's not coming back."

I asked. "What do you think you're here for?" He said, "To get my wife back and my marriage restored."

I responded, "If that happens, what's going to be different? You will still be the same prideful, lustful, sorry-for-yourself person that will not give into lust and porn for a while because of the grief and shame of having committed adultery and nearly losing your wife. You're not here first and foremost to get her back and restore your marriage. You are here to understand what it means to be in a relationship with Christ and for Him to be Lord of your life—all of it! As you walk in this faithfully He will shape and mold you into His disciple and the man and husband that He died for and desires you to be. Then if your wife responds to His work and will in her life and comes back, you will be the husband and man that can make this marriage what God wants it to be. You're here to know Christ above all else."

He agreed with deeper sobs and more tears.

I tell that story for one simple reason. Here was a man and couple that met in Bible college, knew God's Word, and faithfully attended and served in their church. Yet secret sin was prevalent in his life that, once revealed, led to deeper sin and destructive consequences. The response from his wife, while certainly understandable, did not comport with God's Word. Now what God had put together, a man and woman had torn apart.

I'd like to say that the couple is back together and doing well and that this was a rare occurrence in our churches today, but they are not as far as I know. The outcome is far from rare, although it is certainly a lesser occurrence in strong Bible-believing, Christ-centered homes and churches. The common denominator in most every story of broken covenant is that, much like this Bible college-educated, church attending, apparently happy-on-the-outside couple, many do not know and have

He is first in your life, your faith is a laughingstock. We can't continue to display a faith that doesn't put Him first in all things.

In the Battle example, the result is a compromise and likely surrender. This is certainly not the victorious Christian life that His Word speaks of, as so many try to live with a partial or weak faith and claim they are His disciples. By His own words Jesus says that we can't be half-hearted and be His disciples.

OUCH AGAIN! And He's not finished yet.

Jesus goes on to say, "In the same way, those of you who do not give up everything you have cannot be my disciples." (Luke 14:33) How many of us are trying to be His disciples on our own compromised terms when, according to Him, we simply can't be and are not? What must He think of us?

Finally, He closes by stating that those who are trying to live as His disciples on their own terms essentially have no impact in His Kingdom. The impact of their saltiness is worthless.

Let me give you a final paraphrase in context with this passage that I pray will drive the point home and compel all those who call Him Savior to seek and desire to walk with Him as Lord. In essence Jesus is saying, if He's not first in our lives, if we do not count the cost of the calling and commitment, and we do not take up our own cross (i.e., go to the death of our own self and selfish desires) then we are not His disciples. Stated another way: If we are not willing to pay the price, then He is not our Lord and our faith is a mockery to those who observe us. Is it any wonder the culture is not drawn to our modern-day faith and to Christ but rather to our souped-up services designed to attract with little or no accountability and commitment expected? What does your discipleship response to Christ look like?

Look at Paul's instruction here for Godly living, or discipleship in Christ. First we must be brutally honest with ourselves: You (understood pronoun) don't deceive yourself (bold emphasis mine and added). Deception is easy to do in my flesh. Over time His Spirit calls me away from this self-deception to integrity and honesty that is impossible to do in my selfish flesh.

We need to know this or we will deceive ourselves, thinking we are Christ's disciples simply by attending church, giving some money, and serving from time to time, or worse, justifying our sinful thoughts and choices. The former are all good things and we need to do them, but they can be just actions of a fleshly heart seeking favor or attention from others rather than a heart truly surrendered to Christ. Do not deceive yourself. The only way we can know and grow as His disciples is to honestly evaluate our motives, thoughts, and decisions and make sure they are surrendered to His Spirit and will. And as we remain patient and persevere in this honest surrender, we will reap His harvest if we don't give up. That's discipleship.

3) Holy Sacrifice – "Therefore, I urge you, brothers and sisters, in view of God's mercy, to offer your bodies as a living sacrifice, holy and pleasing to God—this is your true and proper worship. Do not conform to the pattern of this world, but be transformed by the renewing of your mind. Then you will be able to test and approve what God's will is—his good, pleasing and perfect will. For by the grace given me I say to every one of you: Do not think of yourself more highly than you ought, but rather think of yourself with sober judgment, in accordance with the faith God has distributed to each of you." (Romans 12:1-3)

Pay attention here as I suspect that many of you, like myself and many others I've shared this with, initially glossed over something incredibly important in this text.

It is clear that Paul, through the Holy Spirit, is calling us as disciples to sacrifice our life to God. What I so often missed was that this is not a salvation command, it is a post-salvation one. Paul is begging us to take what Christ has made "holy and pleasing to God" and surrender it back to God.

It is not our sacrifice that makes us holy and pleasing; it is His sacrifice that has already done that. Our job in fulfilling our calling to discipleship is to take what He has made right in God's eyes and faithfully and sacrificially return it to Him for His Glory. The only difference between the Old Testament sacrifices and what we are called to in the New Testament under the grace of Christ is that we choose to get up and walk away from the altar. Our sacrifice has to be of our own free will, but make no mistake it is what we are called to as His disciples.

Here are four key elements from the John 13 text calling us as His disciples to humble service:

A) Love – Jesus showed them His full and complete love (v. 1). Since God is Love and Christ is God and here He is described as showing them this complete love, as His disciples we should pay close attention to what happens next.

B) Humility – He knew He was from God, returning to God, and God had placed all things in His hands (authority) (v. 3). Remember this is the essence of humility, which is knowing with confidence and contentment who you are in Christ so you can place others above yourself. I asked the Lord several years ago as I was studying and praying through this, "Why would you tell us this about Christ?" Not audibly but very plainly The Spirit placed these thoughts in my mind in line with The Word. "I want you to know that Christ knew Who He was because of what He was getting ready to do." Christ modeled humility. And what did that look like? What was He getting ready to do?

C) Service/Servant's Heart – Jesus got up from the table, removed His robe and put a towel around His waist and began to wash all the disciples' feet (vv. 4-5). This is what loving humility looks like and we will struggle to practice it in our selfish pride if we do not know who we are in Christ. However, He doesn't stop there.

D) Authority – After washing their feet (and His exchange with Peter in vv. 6-11) Jesus does something that should stop us in our tracks when it comes to understanding love, humility, service, and discipleship. He literally calls attention to what He has done and instead of saying, "There, that's love and humble service," He recalls for the 11 remaining disciples that they know Him as Master, Teacher, Rabbi, or Lord, depending on the translation. What do all of these strongly imply? That Jesus is the Authority in their eyes and He confirms it: "You are right, that's what I am." (vv. 12-13)

In one loving act of humble service and with one question and statement, Jesus powerfully tells His disciples, then and now, that love, humility, a servant's heart, and authority cannot be separated in My Kingdom! WOW! This is powerful and speaks to how we should live as His disciples in our homes, churches, and everywhere we are called and placed in this culture and world for His Kingdom and Glory.

every time I tried to put an eating utensil to my mouth my entire arm, side, and back cramped up. It was an extremely painful but lifelong lesson. What did I learn?

I return to the two essential elements needed for good discipline and maturity. Maturity requires discipline and discipline requires manageability and commitment. No matter what we attempt, whether physical as evidenced by my story, mental as evidenced by every test you've taken, or spiritual in growing in Christ, in order to learn and grow in His Truth, we must remain committed to those priorities and principles in His Word. And in order to do that we must make it manageable.

If we had the strength to do it all at once the first time, why would we ever need to go into the weight room? If we already knew His Word and will, why would we ever need to step into His spiritual weight room (or disciplines)?

> We must make it manageable so we can keep the commitment and grow in order to mature as His disciples.

I'm sure you're saying to yourself, "Thanks for the painful visual in that story, but how does this apply to spiritual disciplines?" Great question, and here are the answers with Scriptures for your own study and application. The first six deal with personal discipleship and the last three with discipleship in relationships and fellowship as Christ's Church.

Before I share these, let me explain that those who received the letters in the first century that we've come to know as The Bible would have taken the words written as clear commands to be obeyed from the Apostles and other Holy Spirit-inspired writers. The Scriptures used in calling us to apply the disciplines of discipleship were not given as suggestions. They were, and are, received as commands to be followed in loving obedience (John 14:15). With that said, here are several Scriptures that speak to discipleship and the application in our lives. I include brief explanations and trust The Holy Spirit to compel, encourage, and strengthen you to that loving obedience called for in Scripture and to His Lordship.

God has many commands that all deal with His love for us and us loving Him...He has no demands! They require willful surrender in loving obedience on our part to know all that He has in store for us!

my Redeemer." (Psalm 19:14) For an excellent set of Scriptures exalting God's Word and helping you meditate and reflect on it, read Psalm 119. Read it by the 22 sections of eight verses based on the Hebrew alphabet. It will really help you appreciate and desire God's Word.

4) Communion – Allow me a brief explanation, as this includes not only the very sacred time spent in what many churches call Communion or Eucharist, but also growing in the discipline of communion with other believers in Christ. The first is Paul's recounting of Christ's establishing the Holy Communion: "For I received from the Lord what I also passed on to you: The Lord Jesus, on the night he was betrayed, took bread,

and when he had given thanks, he broke it and said, 'This is my body, which is for you; do this in remembrance of me.' In the same way, after supper he took the cup, saying, 'This cup is the new covenant in my blood; do this, whenever you drink it, in remembrance of me.' For whenever you eat this bread and drink this cup, you proclaim the Lord's death until he comes. So then, whoever eats the bread or drinks the cup of the Lord in an unworthy manner will be guilty of sinning against the body and blood of the Lord. Everyone ought to examine themselves before they eat of the bread and drink from the cup. For those who eat and drink without discerning the body of Christ eat and drink judgment on themselves. That is why many among you are weak and sick, and a number of you have fallen asleep. But if we were more discerning with regard to ourselves, we would not come under such judgment." (1 Corinthians 11:23-31). This second reference is the command to commune and fellowship with others: "They (the believers – mine and added) devoted themselves to the apostles' teaching and to fellowship, to the breaking of bread and to prayer." (Acts 2:42)

5) Sabbath – This requires another brief explanation as you learn and prepare to follow through as Christ's disciples. Under the Old Testament law, breaking the Sabbath was an offense punishable by death. The early Church shifted their focus of worship and all it involved (see Acts 2:42 above) to the first day of the week to commemorate Christ's Resurrection on that day and likely also to allow them as Jews to continue observing the lawful Sabbath. Many believing Jews and some non-Jewish believers continued observing the Jewish Sabbath Day while many non-Jewish believers continued the principle due to the great importance of Sabbath, in God's design and law, but shifted the day to Sunday. The key is to recognize and be obedient to the command of the Sabbath that served two purposes. The first was to recognize that God is Holy and we are not. The second was to recognize that in our unholiness and weakness we would need to recognize our need for rest, put aside pride in our own strength, and observe the Sabbath. "By the seventh day God had finished the work he had been doing; so

times, having all that you need, you will abound in every good work." (2 Corinthians 9:6-8) As we grow and mature, both personally and relationally, as Christ's disciples by the power of His Holy Spirit in the disciplines of His Word and Spirit, we become more like Christ. In doing so the ultimate expression is that the world sees His Truth and love in our individual lives and together as His Body, The Church. If they are not seeing it in us, personally and collectively, then we need to take inventory as to whether or not we are walking as His disciples. All of the aforementioned disciplines come together in the building up and fellowship of Christ's Church.

9) Fellowship/Relationship/Church – "They devoted themselves to the apostles' teaching and to fellowship, to the breaking of bread and to prayer." (Acts 2:42) "And let us consider how we may spur one another on toward love and good deeds, not giving up meeting together, as some are in the habit of doing, but encouraging one another—and all the more as you see the Day approaching." (Hebrews 10:24-25) Discipleship in relationships builds our faithful testimony which spills over into reaching a lost and hurting world with His message in fulfilling the Great Commission. "Then Jesus came to them and said, 'All authority in heaven and on earth has been given to me. Therefore go and make disciples of all nations, baptizing them in the name of the Father and of the Son and of the Holy Spirit, and teaching them to obey everything I have commanded you. And surely I am with you always, to the very end of the age.'" (Matthew 28:18-20)

Without discipline there are no disciples and no discipleship! Without The Holy Spirit we have no spiritual discipline!

I feel so strongly about this that I'm going to repeat what I stated earlier. These are not suggestions or recommendations. These are commands that need to be kept for all those who have counted the cost and desire to walk as Christ's disciples and with Him as Lord.

As promised, I want to show you how you can make and keep this commitment. Don't try to do what I did in the weight room and arrive "fully mature" all at once—we just can't do that. That's why it's called discipleship and requires patience and process over time.

As I shared in the Introduction, I began daily time in God's Word with 15 minutes a day. You may be able to do the same, less or more, but for most who have never practiced these disciplines at all and/or tried to do them all at once and burned out, **here's the simple formula**. Adjust the time to work for you. I promise you, if you will do this, God will honor it, and your time with and growth in Him and His Word will be greatly rewarded.

BEGIN WITH 5 MINUTES EVERY DAY AND DON'T MISS ONE DAY!

This is a wonderful idea that we need to be willing to do, but Christ's strong warning in Matthew 7:21-23 puts this into perspective. One night after one of these sermons on how we can really love our fellow man, I was reflecting on what had been shared and I truly believe The Holy Spirit gave me the following vision.

A Judgment Day Parable...

I was standing in line at Christ's Judgment throne. When it was my turn to approach, He graciously spoke, "Hi, Greg." I was a little taken aback although I shouldn't have been. That may have been my first clue, but I proceeded to pull out the long list of things I'd done in accordance with all the pastors and church instructions to show others how much I loved them.

Two in particular stood out so I exclaimed, "Jesus, check this out. Our pastor told us that to show others Your Love, the next time I was in the drive-thru line to just randomly pay for the person's meal behind me and leave a little for the cashier. I decided to really show them Your Love and paid for three carloads behind me. That was a bit of a financial strain, but I did what I was told to do. Shortly after that my wife and I were on a date night and, being on a tight budget, we went to Outback with a 25% off coupon.

"We were seated at Nina's table. She was a frail, fairly young lady who looked worn-out but smiled and gave us wonderful service. That made it much easier for me to do what I'm going to share with you. We left her a $100 bill on a $40 ticket! Not only did we leave this big tip; I wrote on a napkin and laid it on top of the tip so she'd be surprised when she found it. I did notice that when we gave her the discount coupon her smile faded a bit and I bet she was thinking, "Oh no, another reduced ticket... and tip."

Boy was she in for a surprise due to our showing her Your love. We slipped away from the table but I wanted to linger at a distance to see her reaction and of course to get the satisfaction of having served so wonderfully. She almost missed it.

The wonderful smile turned into a near-snarl as she looked at the napkin, quickly read it, and crumpled it up. Then she saw the $100, but instead of smiling, she began to cry. She un-crumpled the napkin and just looked at it. I didn't fully understand it, but I knew we'd shown her Your love."

"Really?" Jesus asked.

"Of course," I replied, "and there's much more where that came from." I unfolded a list that ran all the way down the "Stairway to Heaven." I was going to show Jesus how much I'd done in serving Him and others, and of course, that I belonged in Heaven.

He interrupted me at this point and said, "Greg, that's enough. I don't need to see or hear any more. However, Greg, you're a sinner and you must depart from me for all of Eternity because you never knew me. We

Nina joyously ran into the Heavenly Kingdom with a huge smile...as I, drifting further into the darkness and torment, yelled out, "But that's Nina. She's the Outback waitress that I helped save. If she gets in then surely so should I!"

But it was too late. I never knew Him and she did. And that's what makes all the difference both in this life and for Eternity.

There are billions of dollars and millions of people, made in God's image, that serve their fellow man every year around the globe as an overflow of their fleshly compassion, but they do not know Jesus as their Lord. Many sit in our churches. Our service must be more than just a fleshly, compassionate response. It must be an overflow of our surrender, sacrifice, and obedience to Christ as Lord as we share His Truth by our lives as His disciples. Otherwise, we risk adding to the multitude that do not know Jesus, as He prophesied in Matthew 7:21-23.

Is He your Savior and Lord? His Word is very clear that He has made the way through Christ. It is also very clear that He has saved you to be in relationship with Him and the only way you can be in that relationship is to know Him as Lord, as His disciple. Don't miss out by claiming Him as Savior and not knowing Him as Lord.

Every other relationship will reflect whether He is Lord of your life or not. You can be assured that He is and that He is blessing you to be a blessing to others as you serve Him and them. That's how discipleship is lived out—in relationships.

STUDY GUIDE
DISCIPLESHIP...OUR RESPONSE TO HIS LORDSHIP

Key Concepts

1) Salvation is free and places us in a relationship with God that we could have in no other way.
2) Discipleship requires commitment and a cost on our part with Christ as Lord.
3) Christ as Lord means that He must take first priority in every part of our life.
4) Being a disciple of Christ requires that I die to my own selfish interests.
5) Honorable submission, honest surrender, holy sacrifice and humble service characterize the life of a disciple of Christ.
6) As Christ's disciple I'm called to sacrifice the life that He saved back to Him.
7) Discipleship requires that I practice personal and relational disciplines found in God's Word and by the power of His Holy Spirit.
8) A disciple of Christ develops and practices habits and disciplines to live wisely and build good relationships in Christ and by The Holy Spirit.
9) Discipleship is first and foremost about knowing, loving, and serving God so that we can then love and serve our fellow man.

Questions

1) How have you been taught to view salvation and discipleship?
2) Is Christ first (Lord) in every part of your life?
3) If so, how are you helping others to know Him? If not, what will you do about it?

*"The answer lies in a personal relationship to Jesus Christ...
We can ever remain powerless, as were the disciples, by trying
to do God's work not in concentration on His power,
but by ideas drawn from our own temperament. We slander
God by our very eagerness to work for Him without knowing
Him...This is your line of service— to see that there
is nothing between Jesus and yourself. Is there?"*

— Oswald Chambers
My Utmost for His Highest

Disguising Godly Relationships

Several years ago, I was asked to speak for the final three weeks of a four-week series at a large men's gathering. The topic was "Men, Lust/Porn and Relationships." Craig Gross of XXX Church kicked off the first week. Usual attendance at this weekly gathering ran about 250-300. During this series there were 450-500 men each week.

After teaching my first week on pursuing a loving relationship with God, I followed up the next week with how to build a Godly, fulfilling marriage and family. I was challenging the men to be sure they were prioritizing their lives, marriage, spouse and family according to God's covenant order (the scope of this book).

In the middle of sharing, The Spirit laid a question on my heart about an upcoming Promise Keepers (PK) conference that was just three weeks away: "How many of you are planning to attend the PK Conference in a couple of weekends?"

Let me just say, I'm a big PK fan, as were many in the group. Nearly two-thirds of the 450+ in attendance excitedly raised their hands showing their commitment to be Godly men. The Spirit immediately prompted me to ask a follow up question. My initial thought was, "REALLY? You want me to ask that?" Yet I knew why He was prompting me to do so. "OK," I silently agreed and took a deep breath...

our day and time—his greatest weapon against, and destroyer of, loving relationships is "porneia" (Greek word from where we get "pornography," rooted in our selfish lustful desires).

I once heard that Hugh Hefner said, "The reason I've been so successful in this business (porn) is because the Church has done such a horrible job with sexuality!" I've searched to no avail to find out if he actually said it. Whether he did or not, the statement is accurate and this must change.

It's not enough for the church to simply speak for marriage, purity, and moral relationships based on God's Word. We must hold Christ followers accountable to this as a priority if we are to see loving relationships across the board. We also must be willing to boldly speak and stand against relational and sexual immorality in all forms and be able to do so with grace, gentleness, and respect. Only then will we see loving relationships, healthy marriages and families, and strong churches.

Much more on this to come.

Loving Relationships vs. Stuff/Success

God's Word calls us to seek His Kingdom and Righteousness first (Matthew 6:33) and to focus on that which is eternal rather than temporal (2 Corinthians 4:18). These commands prompt us to explore what The Holy Spirit means in His Word when He speaks of eternal or Kingdom things to ensure that we understand where we are to invest our lives.

After a thorough search I could find only three things that exist on this temporal earth that are Kingdom in nature. They are: 1) God's Holy Spirit; 2) God's Word and; 3) the souls of human beings. Everything else is temporary and will pass away. Only these three will remain and they all exist for relationship.

My question to you: "What are you doing with His Word, His Spirit, and the lives of those around you? Are you investing in what will last or in that which will someday perish?"

God's Word shows a very clear contrast between His design and desire for loving relationships and the world's attraction to stuff and self at the expense of true relationships. The two words in Scripture that best describe love are "hesed" in Hebrew (Old Testament) and "agape" in Greek (New Testament).

Both words describe God's unconditional, sacrificial, unfailing, selfless lovingkindness (US^2 - His Love is always exponentially toward US!). All expressions of love find their source in His love (1 John 4:19). We call lots of things love that aren't!

On the other hand, "porneia" is the Greek word from which we derive "pornography" and stands for any and all sexual immorality. It goes even further in Scriptural context and includes a sexually immoral mindset evident in sexual sin.

SEXUALITY

Kingdom Currency - Christ as Lord – Agape
- Marriage as One Woman, One Man (Genesis 2:24; Matt. 19:5-6)
- Our bodies as part of Body of Christ, Temple of Holy Spirit
    (I Corinthians 5:13; 6:19)
- Sexual Purity and Blessing (I Corinthians 6:18; Ephesians 5:3)

World's Currency – Satan ("Self") as lord – Porneia
- Depravity of man (all sexual sin) (Romans 1 – emphasis vv. 18-32)
- Lusts of the flesh (Galatians 5:16-19)
- Lust, Sin, Death (James 1:15)

"Flee from sexual immorality ('porneia'). All other sins a person commits are outside the body, but whoever sins sexually, sins against their own body." (1 Corinthians 6:18) (Parentheses mine and added)

Hesed/Agape and Porneia/Lust cannot willingly exist together in your heart. One or the other will win out. Which are you choosing?

Understand that there is a difference between a stronghold and a struggle. A stronghold is something that you have given into. It is set up in your heart and mind, controlling or dictating your thoughts and actions. You have either willingly or subconsciously done so and now live by its hold on you regardless of what you say. You may say you desire God's love in your life but continually choose the lust of the flesh, the lust of the eyes, or the pride of life (1 John 2:15-17) over and over again. This is a stronghold, and porneia is perhaps the strongest.

You can never win and hesed/agape cannot reign in your life if you continue to willingly give in to porneia or any stronghold. You must recognize it, quit deceiving yourself, and surrender it to The Holy Spirit to conquer it by changing your motives, thoughts, decisions, and actions. Otherwise it will cripple and destroy your life and every relationship.

A struggle is something you battle against because you are aware of it and do not desire to have it in your life. For this reason, you may struggle with porneia or any of the lusts of the flesh, lusts of the eyes, or pride of life, but you fight against it. Know that as a Christ follower you already have the victory! Even though you may struggle, you will overcome if you continue to walk in faith—believe in God's overcoming Truth and act accordingly, even when you struggle.

individual meetings with him had revealed that he truly desired to rid himself of this porn "demon" and he had not even attempted to look at anything for nearly four months. I also reassured her that there was still something he was struggling with and that is why she was noticing the frustration and distance. He was not engaging in porn, as the world and enemy would have us see it in active pursuit and participation with videos, magazines, or screens. He had been faithful in that regard.

He was encouraged by my comments to her. However, I looked at him and asked him, "While you're not pursuing porn as defined just now, you are still struggling with the videos and photos that play over and over in your mind. Is that a fair statement?"

He looked down at the floor and nodded his head. It was not easy, but she was reassured that he was not seeking out porn and was willing to walk through that struggle for the porneia in his mind. They would do this by renewing the mind (Romans 12:2), and taking thoughts captive and making them obedient to Christ (2 Corinthians 10:4-5), along with continued accountability and help.

His face softened for the first time in a long time and he shared with her that with The Lord's help and hers, he would be able to get through this and be the husband that she always wanted him to be.

They moved out of state a few years ago, but my last report from them was that they were doing very well and enjoying retirement together in the peace, Love, and Lordship of Jesus Christ.

The Cookie Jar – A Satire on Love

This may come across as corny or silly, but I have so many that come up to me after sharing this—sometimes even months or years later—and share their appreciation for this illustration.

Picture yourself as a child, or maybe as a parent with your children, gathered around the dinner table nearly finished with the meal. The children in the picture are struggling to clean up their plate, so mom or dad grabs a jar out of the pantry and takes the top off. The aroma is intoxicating and even though the children have no idea what aroma or intoxicating means, they want what's in that jar!

Trouble is, mom or dad says, "If you clean up all the green things on your plate you can have one of these." The smell is incredible, so with a few veggies under the table, some in the dog's belly, and a few making their way slowly down the child's throat, the plate is finally clean!

"Gimme, gimme, gimme," say the children and mom or dad lovingly obliges. It's not until later when the carpet is moved and the dog throws up that you realize that not all the green things ended up where you wanted them to as a parent. Nevertheless, some were eaten and you got to give your children a treat and see them fully enjoy it. What parent doesn't want to be a part of that?

The Cookie Jar Explained

Stick with me as I explain. How many of you were born selfless? I hope no one raised his or her hand. How many of you were born selfish? I hope all of you raised your hands. We are all born selfish and that must be overcome in order to love and build good relationships. The natural inclination, as with the cookie jar, is that once we've found something we like we want more of it with no desire to share.

While you can do cookies that way as a selfish person, at least until you run out, you can't do relationships in this manner. We have to be taught to be selfless, and if we are not or we hold onto our selfish nature, it will show up in any and every relationship. What does that look like? If you're still not putting together the satire of The Cookie Jar, here it is.

I've seen numerous couples in relationship and even walking down the wedding aisle with their imaginary cookie jars tucked under their outside arms. They've learned this is "love:" "I'll give you one cookie if you give me two."

Literally, I've seen this over and over. People are seldom, if ever, taught that the only way Love really works—sticking with our Cookie Jar analogy—is when we learn to say, "Here, you can have all my cookies. That's what I think of you, whether you give me any cookies or not." Obviously if you find someone not willing to share or give of themselves it's not likely they are ready for a loving relationship.

Eventually you'll figure out that those who never learned to love don't share or give away their cookies without demanding more in return than were given. You realize that this won't work. Over time the one who demands more than they give will eventually realize the person they've demanded from has run out long before they did—so they move on to the next person...and the next cookie jar.

Here's the bottom line of The Cookie Jar seen from the perspective of God's hesed/agape love. Love is not give and take. Love is give, period! If I never learn to give and become selfless, if I only learn to take and demand or exact an exchange that's at least equal but preferably in my favor, then I will never know love.

Only when I learn to die to my selfishness and be willing to unconditionally give myself for the sake of others will I ever be able to love. This is a lifelong pursuit.

That's what Jesus did. He said, "Here, you can have all that I am (all my cookies). I give my all to and for you." He doesn't demand or coerce, He just loves. The only way we can know that is to know Him and learn to love as He does.

With regard to dating, porneia/lust and love, remember that you must first learn and begin to die to self in order to love. Then, not only can you love, but you can also help others know what it is and recognize it in others. No matter what you see in another, no matter how "hot" they are

After a few weeks of this couple dating and seeing each other nearly every day, she explained that the following week she would have to spend most of her time working due to the timing and demands. She would not be able to see him and it was legit. He understood, or so he thought.

On Tuesday evening of that week he decided to surprise her by simply stopping by her condo and leaving her a dozen roses. How romantic! He wished her well and let her know he was thinking of and praying for her week and left the roses.

On Friday evening he showed up fully expecting her to be ready to go out on another date as the week had passed and she was free, in his mind; but she had promised to spend that night with her daughter.

She was surprised to find him there when she opened the door. There had been no communication, simply expectation and assumption. She explained that this evening was going to be spent with her daughter and he graciously said he understood and left.

We met the next week as usual and he recounted the whole story of the week—the roses, the Friday night "rejection"—and as it had festered in his mind, he'd become quite agitated. He couldn't believe that she "stood him up" even though there was no date arranged.

We talked briefly about the communication side of things and he understood that his assumptions and expectations were guiding his emotional responses. He was still frustrated and said to me, "I can't believe after I left her alone all week—except for the roses and to tell her I was praying—that she would turn me down for a date on Friday."

We'd been talking, as mentioned, about relationship, love, communication, and expectations. I truly believe The Holy Spirit laid the next question on my mind so I said to him, "Let me ask you one question."

"Sure," he said.

"Who'd you buy the roses for?" I asked.

"For her, of course," he retorted with a faint hint of disgust.

I repeated the question and he slowly and a little more thoughtfully repeated the same answer.

"I'll ask one more time," I said, "Who'd you really buy the roses for?"

He thought about it and it hit him, based on what we'd been discussing and how things had gone. He looked at me and slowly and resignedly said, "I bought them for me, didn't I?"

"Now you're getting it. Friday night proved that Tuesday night you were being nice so you'd get something in return," I said.

That's the culture's description and modus operandi when it comes to so-called love. But that's really lust because we do things with the full expectation of a return. God's love, agape, is selfless and reaches out and serves regardless of the response or return. It's hard to grasp in our selfish flesh, but the love He gives to us and desires for us to share

Isn't it interesting that as Caleb was viewing the boat, the item he was sure would fully satisfy him, that the porn temptation popped up? The selfish state of his mind (the movie has made it clear that the boat was an idol for him) made it easier for the enemy to draw him in. He wisely chose to fight against it and won the battle.

Now let's apply that to King David. I ask for some leeway here as I'm going to "fill in some gaps" in the story that completely fit the context and may help us see how the self-absorbed mind makes it so much easier to fall into temptation and sin.

Second Samuel 11:1 says, "in the spring, at the time when kings go out to battle," and then proceeds to tell us that King David decided to send his general and army out to clean up some unfinished business in war while he lounged around his palace. There's nothing particularly sinful about his choice, but it does give us insight into his mind. He was thinking about David rather than his army. Otherwise he would have gone with them as kings do.

The Bible gives us no indication whatsoever that he stayed home for any particular reason and especially not to look for naked women. One evening he's walking on his palace rooftop and sees a beautiful woman bathing. He's stricken with her and immediately asks his servant to go ask who she is.

Here's where I interject David's potential and likely thought patterns based on his self-absorbed decision to stay home and take it easy rather than go to battle with his men. What story do you think David may have crafted in his mind as his servant is inquiring about the beautiful woman?

Maybe it goes something like this…"I can't wait for my servant to return and tell me this woman's name and even more importantly that she's single and available." I mean initially if he's going to enter into a relationship he wants it to be done the right way and I'm sure he's thinking this is all going to work out great.

The problem occurs when the servant returns to report that Bathsheba is not only married but it is to one of David's top men, Uriah the Hittite. Now David has to figure out whether he's going to continue with the story in his mind where this woman is his to have or follow God's Truth and leave her to her husband.

Once again, the choice reveals where the mind is leading. David sends for her and sleeps with her. Seems like he's gotten away with it until Bathsheba sends a report that she's pregnant! It couldn't be her husband's baby as he's off fighting David's war.

David schemes to bring Uriah home so he'll sleep with his wife and cover it up. Uriah does the noble thing for both nights and does not sleep with his wife because that would not be right with the other warriors out to battle.

God's Love as Painful Truth

In Mark 10, Jesus is pursued by another young man. "As He was setting out on a journey, a man ran up to Him and knelt before Him, and asked Him, 'Good Teacher, what shall I do to inherit eternal life?' And Jesus said to him, 'Why do you call Me good? No one is good except God alone. You know the commandments, 'DO NOT MURDER, DO NOT COMMIT ADULTERY, DO NOT STEAL, DO NOT BEAR FALSE WITNESS, DO NOT DEFRAUD, HONOR YOUR FATHER AND MOTHER.' And he said to Him, 'Teacher, I have kept all these things from my youth up.' **Looking at him, Jesus felt a love for him** and said to him, 'One thing you lack: go and sell all you possess and give to the poor, and you will have treasure in heaven; and come, follow Me.' But at these words he was saddened, and he went away grieving, for he was one who owned much property." (vv. 17-22 NASB) (Bold text mine and added for emphasis)

I've heard dozens of sermons on the rich young ruler, and one thing I've never heard explained with any clarity was the phrase in verse 21: "Looking at him, Jesus felt a love for him." As I studied and prayed about this, fully believing that Jesus/God always loved perfectly, I asked The Spirit to show me what's going on here. It's easy to see Christ's love for the leper, as it is likely what every one of us would have done had we the power and opportunity to do so. We would have healed him and given him back his life.

The love for the rich young ruler that Jesus displayed is puzzling. If we're honest with ourselves as believers, and especially as modern-day church-going believers, we struggle with Jesus' response to him. Here the Greek word is "**agapao**," rooted in "agape" or God's selfless, sacrificial love. "Agapao" is used 110 times in the New Testament (appearing 47 times in the Gospels) and "agape" appears 106 times in the New Testament (8 times in the Gospels)* and every time it deals with love for others that esteems them above self—whether it is a family member, neighbor, stranger, or enemy. *The NAS New Testament Greek Lexicon

What in the world is God trying to tell us? First of all, I think He is teaching us that His love expresses itself perfectly every time. In the case of these two men, one expression is with heartfelt compassion and the other in heart-spoken Truth. But I think there's a second thing that The Holy Spirit is trying to teach us through the choice of words used: the deeper word defined as love with the rich young ruler is "agapao" and is stronger than the description of love as compassion. While we must teach and model compassion, sharing truth is the most loving thing we can do and we must present it completely regardless of how those who hear it may respond. Jesus knew the rich young man would reject His loving truth, but the greatest and most perfect act of love was to tell Him the Truth that alone could set Him free.

6) Second Command, Part 2 – Love your neighbor as you love yourself (Matthew 22:39; Mark 12:31) Loving my neighbor (all others), continuing with priority and order:

   - Marriage – Only covenant/highest human relationship; as one in Christ this new "disciple" takes priority over either spouse (Matthew 19:4-6)

   - Spouse – Reflects Christ and His Bride (Ephesians 5:21-27; 32-33)

   - Children – God builds His family with Godly offspring (Malachi 2:13-16; Ephesians 6:4)

   - Family members (I Timothy 3:5; 5:4, 8)

   - Friends/Family of God (Galatians 6:10; 1 Peter 2:17); also remembering Christ's words regarding family (Luke 8:20-22)

   - Others/Worldly Acquaintances (Romans 12:18, 21; Galatians 6:10)

   - Enemies (Matthew 5:11, 44; Luke 10:30-37; Romans 12:14)

Here's the power of what God has given us in His Covenant Order and prioritizing how we are to love. Priorities, as previously stated, reveal who is Lord/lord in our life. Priorities also order our decision-making and our relationships. Our time and schedules should reflect this. As we walk with Christ as Lord and in line with His Word, we can order our thoughts, lives, and decisions to show the love we are given and called to share as His disciples in a way that it brings us His Shalom or wholeness and peace.

We will have to sacrifice; that is what love does, as we've established in Christ's life and teaching and in God's Word and commands for us to love as He loved us. This is love and this is how we are to build the relationships together as His disciples to grow His Church and His Kingdom.

Here is one final note in tying together discipleship and relationship. I've never seen this happen in practice, although I've heard it talked about. If discipleship is lived out in relationship and relationships are formed and matured through loving discipleship, then we should follow God's Covenant Order when it comes to discipling believers in Christ.

Leaders, how often do we place, implicitly or explicitly (and I've seen and heard countless examples of both), the needs of the local fellowship and community above that of personal maturity in Christ and marriages and families within the church? How often have we encouraged, cajoled, and even lovingly manipulated members to sign up and serve to show others in the church and community how much God loves them by how much we love them, having spent little or no time discipling them in the greatest commands...worship and love God first, know and love who we are in Christ, then we are equipped and maturing as we love others?

*"To be faithful in every circumstance
means that we have only one loyalty,
and that is to our Lord...We will be loyal
to work, to service, to anything, but
do not ask us to be loyal to Jesus Christ...
The idea is not that we do work for God,
but that we are so loyal to Him that
He can do His work through us —
'I reckon on you for extreme service,
with no complaining on your part and
no explanation on Mine.' God wants to
use us as He used His own Son."*

— Oswald Chambers
My Utmost for His Highest

4) What do you see in your life that is helping to grow your relationships?
5) What is hindering or harming your relationships?
6) Are you involved in porneia? Do you have an accountability partner?
7) What do your decisions say about how you're prioritizing your relationships?
8) Do you have someone to disciple you in your relationship with The Lord and with others?
9) Are you discipling anyone in their relationship with The Lord and with others?

Discussion

1) How do you think your discipleship affects your relationships? How do your relationships help or hinder your walk with The Lord?
2) Do the stories of Christ's perfect love toward the leper and rich young ruler help you understand His love or muddy the waters?
3) Where would your spouse say you rate him/her in the priority of relationships? Your children? The Church?

Action Item

Find (or form) a small group with the focus of growing together in Christ and holding each other accountable to do so.

"*So they called Rebekah and asked her, "Will you go with this man?" "I will go," she said.* (Genesis 24:58)

"And she said, 'I will go.'" Those words are the answer to Eliezer's prayer. Rebekah felt the thrill which always passes through any pure young heart in the presence of a saint. A soul's trust in a saint in the providence of God is something more precious even than love. Few of us know anything about it because we are too sordidly selfish; we want things for ourselves all the time. Eliezer had only one conception, loyalty to his master, and in the providence of God he brought Rebekah straight to Isaac. **This marriage, like all true marriages, concerns the Kingdom of God."**

— Oswald Chambers
My Utmost for His Highest

(Bold is mine and added)

A few years later two similar situations occurred just a few years apart. I was asked to be a national spokesperson for an expanding nonprofit company. At the time, our three children (we added our beautiful daughter, Haidyn, in 1999) were elementary age or younger. My response was simple: "How can I help raise my children if I'm traveling all over the country?" The founder and CEO replied, "I thought you might say that, but we had to try anyway."

The second inquiry for the same position was offered to me again a few years later with Lansing just entering middle school and Harrison and Haidyn in elementary school. This time they asked: "Did you know that you could fly to two-thirds of the continental US and back home in a day?" As much as I would have enjoyed that position and Ami and I would have loved to travel around the country, my answer again reflected the priorities that had guided me in my walk with The Lord. I responded with a question: "How does leaving at 6 AM and arriving back home at 9 PM or later honor my marriage and wife or help raise my children?"

"We knew you were going to say that but we had to try again."

I closed that conversation with this simple statement of faith that I knew I could rely on: "If The Lord desires me to be in that or any similar position, then He will show me the time and place. And if not, then I'm fine with what I've chosen."

Some readers may struggle with my choices and some may even be angry. Please know I'm not condemning anyone who has made or may make a different choice. I'm simply sharing with you why I made the choices based on my understanding of God's Covenant Order and how He has blessed us in our marriage and family. I would not trade that for anything.

I can tell you that I have counseled hundreds who have made different decisions in similar situations and have sat in my office with great regret for what they sacrificed. Remember, relationships in the Kingdom, or the stuff of this world, at some point there will be sacrifice of one or the other. Your choices and actions determine which is sacrificed no matter how you may claim, "I did it for my family."

Marriage Should Be Honored By All

Most Bible scholars would agree that Hebrews is one of the two deepest theological letters, along with Romans, in all of Scripture. I find it very interesting that near the end of this profound text on Christ completely fulfilling the Old Covenant in the New Covenant, we find this verse, "Marriage should be honored by all, and the marriage bed kept pure, for God will judge the adulterer and all the sexually immoral." (Hebrews 13:4)

Let's see—all means all, right? So The Holy Spirit is not just saying that all those who are married, have been married, or are planning on getting married, should honor marriage. All means all!

The goal of every relationship is to imitate Christ. The only way we can do this is if He is our Lord. That makes discipleship the key to every good relationship and especially the most important earthly one—marriage.

Are you content to place other worldly relationships ahead of your marriage? Or are you making it the priority as God sees it? You will be blessed if you do.

God has shown us how much He values marriage in His design and highest desire for its sanctity, His command that all should honor it, and its reflection of His image and our relationship with Him. With this in mind let's connect the dots with regard to His Lordship, our discipleship relationship with Him, and all loving relationships, finding the highest expression in the marriage relationship.

🔑 **Submission** is the key found in what we are called to do in honoring one another in relationships and particularly in marriage. Ephesians 5:21-25: "Submit to one another out of reverence for Christ. Wives, submit yourselves to your own husbands as you do to the Lord. For the husband is the head of the wife as Christ is the head of the church, his body, of which he is the Savior. Now as the church submits to Christ, so also wives should submit to their husbands in everything. Husbands, love your wives, just as Christ loved the church and gave himself up for her."

We must learn to first love God and, out of honor for Christ, we are called to submit to one another. Wives are commanded to submit to their husbands. This is not a command to the husband to make his wife submit. This is a command to the wife to willingly choose to submit to her husband because she has already submitted to Christ and learned to love God with all she is.

Husbands are called to submit in love and servant-leadership, literally to submit or surrender his life for his wife just as Christ did for His Bride, The Church. Again, wives, this is not a command to you to make your husband love you. It is a command to husbands to be obedient to Christ in daily choosing to love our wife because we have first submitted to Christ and learned to love God with all we are.

I mentioned earlier in this book that many of these principles would be repeated and would take on deeper meaning as we learn and apply God's Truth to the highest of human relationships in marriage so that we can build Godly families, and from these, the loving relationships that are His Church!

Years ago The Spirit revealed one of the most profound teachings and I have taught it faithfully ever since. It has changed countless husbands and, in the process, marriages (and wives) for His glory. Remember every marriage is intended to reflect His image and glorify Him and also, husbands, that we are the Christ figure in our marriage!

In my prayer and study, I was challenged to go beyond the obvious question, "Husbands, would you take a bullet (die) for your wife?" This is a question most pastors, Christian counselors, or marriage therapists ask reiterating to husbands the command for them "to love their wife and give up their life for her as Christ did the Church." As I thought through this The Spirit took me to Philippians 2:5-8. I didn't get it at first, but the more I prayed and meditated it became clear what He was prompting me to teach in line with His Word.

The Apostle Paul, who wrote both Ephesians and Philippians under the inspiration and guidance of The Holy Spirit, was giving instructions to husbands as to what it truly cost Christ to "lay down His life for His

need to lay down our lifestyles and place the needs and desires of our wife above our own. This has to hold true because had Jesus not surrendered His lifestyle in heaven first, then He could not have become fully God and fully man and His death on The Cross (what we always equate with "giving up our life for our wife") would have meant nothing.

In order for Jesus' life and death on earth to accomplish anything He first had to give up His lifestyle in heaven.

I know it's not easy, but it's good because it is what He has called us to and He did nothing less than model it for us!

Now we are beginning to grasp what love truly is and how we can love our wife, family, and all others, which is our third command and key.

3) Love Others As You Love Yourself! (Matthew 22:39; Mark 12:31) Are you beginning to see God's design for loving relationships? As shared earlier, we cannot fully love others unless we have first begun to grow in our love for God and for ourselves. This should be paramount in how we make disciples. Teach and train first to love God,and love who we are in Christ so we can then love others and show them His love. As we submit to Christ and others, humble ourselves, and place others before self, we are developing the same attitude and heart as Christ, allowing us to love others with the third key:

Servant's Heart – we see this when Jesus washes His disciples' feet and then instructs them to do the same for others in John 13:12-17. "When he had finished washing their feet, he put on his robe and returned to his place. 'Do you understand what I have done for you?' he asked them. 'You call me 'Teacher' and 'Lord,' and rightly so, for that is what I am. Now that I, your Lord and Teacher, have washed your feet, you also should wash one another's feet. I have set you an example that you should do as I have done for you. Very truly I tell you, no servant is greater than his master, nor is a messenger greater than the one who sent him. Now that you know these things, you will be blessed if you do them.'"

Remember from our earlier teaching on this text in John 13 that this is the culmination where love (v.1), humility (v.3), serving (vv.4-5), authority (v.13) and now discipleship (vv. 14-17) come together. This is what Kingdom relationships are to look like...and the highest of those is Marriage.

That brings us back to Ami's call. She explained what we'd talked about many times before, that whenever I didn't show up at or near the appointed time, distrust would rear its ugly head. This happened too many times as I got caught up in getting things in order and failed to give her a call and let her know.

She said, "If you would just give me a call and let me know what's going on and reassure me that all is well, it would help me a lot."

Now, as I've shared this with many men and couples, the typical response in our pride as men is to think, "She's just checking up on me and I don't need another Momma! She just needs to trust me." I have to admit that knowing I was doing nothing wrong or worthy of distrust, I entertained the same thoughts and response.

However, before I said anything, I said a quick prayer and in that moment The Holy Spirit simply prompted me to think, "Pride or humility? Your choice."

I asked Ami what she needed and she said, "If you'd just call once or twice a day, especially if something happens and you know your schedule is going to change, that would help me so much."

Simple, right? I either bow my back and tell her to get over it and trust me, or I do something to help her build more trust in me. The Holy Spirit's prompting came to me again and it really was simple. Pride puts the burden on her and would continue to lead to distrust. Humility put the burden on me to do all I could to show her that she could trust me.

I began the next day and have not missed a day of calling or texting her in the 25-plus years since. Distrust faded and trust became her default as God directed me to think of her above myself and I obeyed instead of giving into my pride. With that trust came an ever-growing peace in our marriage and family. Totally worth it!

I close this with what I share with every guy that I counsel on this: "You can choose to think, 'I don't need another Momma,' (every one of them shares that thought), or you can humbly do what's best for your wife and marriage. Two to four minutes of calls or texts each day will mean two to four hours of peace each evening that builds more and more over the course of your marriage as long as you are being honest and trustworthy. Or you can choose to put the burden on her and watch the tension and distrust build each evening and throughout your marriage. Seems like a 'no-brainer' to me, but it's your choice."

A Marriage Parody on Loving Servant-Leadership

In the Love & Lordship events I share this parody, "Clothes Basket on the Stairs." Before I do I remind both husbands and wives that it may not be a clothes basket for you so be sure to fill in the blank so that you will not miss the lesson.

"Clothes Basket on the Stairs"

A couple has been married about five years. The husband comes home one evening from work and as he ascends the steps he sees a clothes basket sitting on them. He wonders to himself, "Hmm, what in the world is that?"

He walks on up the stairs and gets ready for the evening.

About four years later he encounters the basket on the stairs again. This time he says to himself, "That's a clothes basket. Somebody's doing laundry."

Another three years pass and he comes home and finds the clothes basket once again on the stairs. "This must be my wife doing these clothes. She's really good as this is the third time in 12 years that she's done the laundry. She's awesome." So he shouts up the steps, "Honey, thanks for doing the laundry."

Suddenly there's a "thud" and he rushes up the stairs to find his wife passed out on the floor. "Hmm," he wonders again. And then he changes clothes and gets ready for the evening.

Now it's been nearly 13 years of marriage and he comes home one evening to an empty house. He once again sees the basket full of clean clothes on the stairs and thinks, "Wow, my wife is incredible. She's done laundry four times in 13 years! She's gooooood!"

He decides to take the clothes up the stairs and put them all away himself. His wife comes in after carting the kids around to piano, soccer, drama and karate practice on top of the long day of cleaning the house and yes, the clothes. She drops into bed and immediately falls asleep giving no thought to the missing clothes basket on the stairs.

All is well until the next morning when figurative fireworks explode as no one can find any of their clothes. Shirts are where pants should be. Pants are in with underwear. Bras are with blouses and everyone is running late.

I'm sure you get the point.

When I finish this parody, I ask the wives what it would mean for their husband to be involved in such a way that there would be no fireworks? Usual answers include, "It means he cares." "It means he loves us." Or, "It means he's thinking of us."

Then I ask them "Why?" Most struggle or have to think about this. I

and moved beyond the emotions, hurt feelings, accusations, or "fill in the blank." Stay with me here.

There is a process. It's just that forgiveness is not that process. Emotions and feelings associated with the offense or violation require time and processing. Forgiveness, on the other hand, is a choice that you can make immediately because it's what God has done for each of us who believe in Christ. And He says that we absolutely must forgive.

According to His Word, forgiveness is a mandate—a command (Ephesians 4:32). The only thing that Jesus repeated after His "Model Prayer" or "The Lord's Prayer" (Matthew 6:9-13) is the issue of forgiveness (vv. 14-15). If you do not forgive, then your Heavenly Father will not forgive you. If I want to know His forgiveness, then I must forgive everyone, period. I'm pretty sure you agree that we want and need His forgiveness.

This is the subtle deception that has entered into our counseling and wreaked havoc on countless marriages, families, and relationships. If I'm not ready (i.e., don't feel like it), then I should allow time to "process" my feelings before I forgive. **This ties forgiveness to our feelings rather than His Truth.** I don't see that concept in God's Word. Again, His grace is amazing, but it never compromises His Truth to any degree.

If you are willing to be deceived and allow feelings to trump God's Truth, then you give the enemy territory and ammunition. He will use your flesh through your emotions to kill, steal, and destroy you and others in the struggle and process. It's not a good ride or a gentle landing.

On the other hand, this Truth has helped many couples and people: If you are obedient to God to forgive, choosing to do so by His grace in and through you, then His Spirit and Truth will guide you through the emotional pain and process.

Know you are now forgiven and free in Christ as you give the same to others!

While forgiveness or unforgiveness is tied directly to trust they are not the same. If we are willing to forgive, then we can rebuild trust but it takes time. Even Jesus did not trust others because He knew what was in their heart (John 2:24). In less than three years after this text, because He had taught and modeled truth, love and forgiveness for them, He entrusted His life story, The Gospel, to 120 men and women in an upper room (Acts 2:1-4). His forgiveness had allowed His life to be formed in them and that is what He was trusting.

We can do the same in our marriage and in all relationships, including in His Church, if we are willing to walk as His disciples, forgive others and learn to live as He did, and begin to see His life in them.

Unconditional Love & Marriage

Marriage is based on Commitment and Unconditional Love. Here's a simple and great definition for love, based on Christ's for His Bride

We made all our plans for travel and childcare, got our shots and passports, and took off for Cameroon for the conference in November 2010. We had a wonderful week and over 1100 people attended the conference.

We closed out on a Thursday night and I taught on the information laid out directly above on marriage, divorce, remarriage, and adultery.

We went sightseeing on Friday, as we were to end the week with a Pastor's conference on Saturday. Approximately 50 pastors and spouses showed up on Saturday and I spoke about taking the message to a lost and hurting world based on the Love & Lordship principles presented in this book.

As we wrapped up the pastor's conference and the week, the gentleman who had been our chauffeur and my interpreter the entire week approached me. I could see he was visibly moved as he took my hand and began to speak with tears in his eyes and a lump in his throat.

He said, "I want to thank you for coming to Cameroon and speaking God's Truth to us. My wife and I were set free on Thursday night after God's message through you. We've never had an American pastor speak it so plainly, graciously and boldly. We've never had an American pastor even share this truth."

Needless to say, I was both encouraged and disheartened. Encouraged personally, but disheartened by the reality that tough issues are often ignored or soft-pedaled in our churches in America today.

He went on to share that after the teaching he went home and told his wife that he needed to pray with her and ask her forgiveness. She asked him why and he said, "I now know that I've committed adultery." She gasped and he reassured her it was because his first wife had left him and he had now married her, his second wife.

They knelt and prayed for over an hour. When they stood up with tears in their eyes they looked at each other and said, "I feel like a weight has just been lifted from our shoulders and we can now truly become one and do all that God has called us to do."

He thanked me again and left as I stood there, tears now filling my eyes. I had goose bumps all over me.

Everyone else had left except for the pastor who had invited us and coordinated the entire conference. He approached me and asked if the interpreter had shared his story with me. I confirmed that he had and told him how awesome it was to see God show up in that way.

The pastor asked, "Do you know who he is?" I answered, in a matter of fact tone, "He's the chauffeur and interpreter."

He said, "He is the president of the entire Western African Association of Churches. Did you see...?"

Before he could finish I said, "I know what you're going to say. All week long all the other pastors had kept him literally at arm's length with

STUDY GUIDE
MARRIAGE: IN GOD'S IMAGE

Key Concepts

1) In God's design, every marriage is a covenant elevating this to the most important of all human relationships.
2) Marriage is the union of differences. Communication is at the core of Unity.
3) God's design for the marriage covenant is a lifetime commitment.
4) Two pairs of **P.A.N.T.S.** essential for Marriage.
   - **P**roper **A**uthority **N**eeded **T**o **S**ucceed
   - **P**roper **A**ttitude **N**eeded **T**o **S**erve
5) Marriage always reflects on Christ and His Bride, The Church, and on His Gospel.
6) Three Keys to Agape Marriage:
   1) Submission; 2) Humility; 3) Servant's Heart.
7) Forgiveness is mandatory. Trust is earned. These go together but they are not the same thing.
8) Unconditional (Agape) Love = Give 100%; Expect 0! Don't let unmet expectations define you, your spouse or your relationship
9) Meeting each others' needs requires daily dying to self through communication and submission in humility, integrity, and purity. See Marriage Activity below.

Key Questions

1) What is the connection between Love and Respect, service and authority?
2) How can you practice building great relationships and an "agape marriage?"
3) What does unconditional mean? What's the closest you've come to experiencing unconditional love/respect? What's the best you've done in giving it?
4) Why is forgiveness so important? Why is Trust so important?
5) What does it take to really meet someone else's needs?

Notice that women's top need is affection or love, which aligns with God's command for husbands to meet that need by loving their wives. Notice also that men's top need is sex. Respect, the Biblically commanded need to be met by wives, drops to #5. I have to add here that every single time I've sat with couples there are numerous issues but the underlying problem ALWAYS for the husband is lack of respect from his wife.

My encouragement to men is two-fold: 1) Intentionally move Respect to the top of the list and oh, by the way, if you're looking for ways to earn her respect, look at her list (even though she is commanded and should give you that respect anyway, it's always good to strive to be a man who is deserving of that respect); 2) Submit to her as a servant-leader and ask her to share her greatest need and how you can meet it. Work through each need alternating back and forth until they become habit.

Caution: None of this will come naturally. Think about that. If it did you'd already be doing these things. Both of you will need to pray and rely on the power of The Holy Spirit to give you the initiative and strength to do this by faith. However, I assure you, if you're willing to commit to and intentionally invest in your spouse and marriage you'll be blessed beyond anything you've ever experienced!

> "Marriage and family is both the building blocks, and a reflection, of Christ's Church."

"Behold, children are a gift of the LORD,
the fruit of the womb is a reward. Like arrows in the
hand of a warrior, so are the children of one's youth."

(Psalm 127:3-4 NASB)

My prayer and my hope above all else with this book, is to encourage everyone, but especially those who call Christ Lord, to recognize God's Divine Covenant order from Creation to Christ's return. I pray that you'll be willing, as His disciples, to live it out first in your marriages and families in order to strengthen His Church and build His Kingdom accordingly.

This book is the message The Lord has laid on my heart, and I've been sharing it for over 25 years. It has helped hundreds, if not thousands, to walk in His Divine order, see the blessing in their lives and homes, and be a blessing in His Church and beyond. That's His design, plan, and purpose from Genesis to Revelation and it begins in the Home.

Dennis Rainey, founder of FamilyLife, one of the best marriage and family organizations in the world today, said this, "Every family is a little church." Marriage is certainly implied and intended in his quote. In line with God's Word and order, if we are not doing the job in our little churches (marriages and families), then it matters little how much we're doing in our "big" churches. God is faithful to use our sincere efforts but if we will follow His design, I truly believe He has much more in store for our lives and He can and will use us to ignite His Church and impact a lost and dying world!

"There is no doubt that it is around the family and the home
that all the greatest virtues, the most dominating virtues of
human society, are created, strengthened, and maintained."

— Winston Churchill

> "What can you do to promote world peace?
> Go home and love your family."
> — Mother Teresa

What he shared next was a far too common occurrence in our culture and churches today. He said that his relationship with his soon-to-be ex-wife, finally after nearly six years, was not good at all. He revealed that while he had his own place he was living with another woman who had a young special needs child.

I asked about church and he said they had raised their children in church and continued to attend. As a matter of fact, that's where he'd met his live-in and her child. While things were awful with his wife, all was great with his live-in girlfriend and her child. He told how wonderful it was to help out with her child, how much good it was doing, and that they continued to attend church every week together.

The veil had been removed. Here was a man who had decided to divorce his wife, and though the divorce was not final, live with another woman and justify it because they had met in church, and he was helping her with her special needs child. As we talked further it became clear that he was sure that God was okay with this arrangement because he was helping her out and it was so good for her child.

I looked him directly in the eye and said, "Sympathy does not change God's Truth or our need for repentance. You told me you came to me because of what I'd shared about integrity. I'm telling you that you are not living with integrity."

I then asked him what his boys thought of all of this. He said he really noticed that things had gone from bad to worse when he basically moved in and took on this "new family." I reminded him of what I'd shared when we first met about being straightforward.

"You have asked me how you can help continue to raise your boys up with proper discipline and keep their respect. I will tell you that you can continue to practice what we talked about the previous week regarding discipline and clear communication and consequences. But as long as you are not walking in integrity and purity then it is going to be extremely difficult to accomplish the discipline and respect you desire from your boys." He looked puzzled.

I went on to explain that the first thing he needed to do was to break away from his live-in and live according to God's Word in his own life. I explained further that his older teen son clearly knew what was going on and likely so did his younger teen son. Finally I said that this would likely continue because his younger son was mimicking his older brother's actions and disrespect because he was not seeing someone worthy of respect in his father.

I reminded him that his older son was a young man now and likely would continue to pull away unless his dad changed his lifestyle and gave him someone he could look up to. The younger son would probably continue to follow suit.

There is an ancient proverb that reads, "Bend a tree when it is young." This is an excellent interpretation and explanation of Proverbs 22:6 (NASB) for two reasons. First of all, bending a tree requires ongoing attention and effort just as children do. You can't just bend it once and expect it to stay in place. With children, as is strongly implied in the Hebrew text, we as parents must take the time to get to know them, their personality, strengths and weaknesses, and teach and train them in character consistently over time and be there to help them navigate the struggles and trials. This can't be done with occasional gifts of time, money, or stuff. It requires our time and presence. One of the greatest deceptions from the pits of hell is, "Quality time equals quantity time." A father or parent who has fallen for that lie has damaged many a child! Second, one of the greatest recipes for rebellion is to give the disciplines or guidelines for developing character and then be a father or parent who does not walk in the integrity of those disciplines and/or only shows up to reward or punish as it is called for. Far too many children have been the victims of a parent who comes home from work or the road only to administer punishment and demand obedience without being present to model that behavior. Rules – relationships = rebellion! Parents, train your children to walk in the way they should go by first walking that path yourself.

Monte Wilkinson, Lead Minister at Northeast Christian Church, Lexington, KY, was in our wedding and I consider him a good friend. He shared a wonderful maxim with me when he found out we were expecting our first child: "Children are the greatest blessing and greatest burden all rolled into one." I not only found this to be true but have elaborated on it with many in my conferences and counseling. God's Word declares that children are a reward or heritage from The Lord (Psalm 127). If we only see the burden, then we miss the joys of His blessing to us. Scripture also declares that there is a burden in the responsibility of training them up in The Lord (Proverbs 22:6; Ephesians 6:4). If we only looking for blessings, then we miss the lessons and needed pruning in our lives and in our children's as well.

Let me share with you five ways that we can exasperate or frustrate our children and later I'll give some insights as to how we can build them up beyond being careful and reversing the following.

The Church Prioritized

The first father/grandfather was in his mid-70s and retired from a very prominent position in the community. He had been a deacon and an elder at a rapidly growing church. I had known him for years and he asked if I remembered his children. I replied that I did and he simply stated with tears streaming down his cheeks, "Greg, we did exactly what you described in your teaching with regard to making the church the most important thing in our life and family. You've made it clear from Scripture that in God's order the church is to benefit and grow from the priority relationships of marriage and family. When these are either a façade or missing the church becomes just an institution rather than a fellowship of believers in loving relationship because we have not shown our children those relationships where it matters most. We spent most of our time going to and from church functions—for their sake."

He went on to say, "We had a good home," to which I fully agreed. "But, we spent most of our time doing church without knowing and showing Christ." He paused, very choked up and with tears flowing freely said, "Because we did exactly as you described, showing up at every function, making our kids go to every youth group, retreat and event, which they fully enjoyed, but something was clearly missing. Now neither of our children attend church and our grandchildren have never darkened the door of a church."

I shared with him, "I believe you do have a good marriage and home that just got sidetracked as so many have. Continue to show your children and grandchildren the agape love of God in your marriage and with them, and trust they will return and in doing so know more fully what it means to live in His Love and Lordship."

He hugged me and thanked me.

The Church Comes First

As I watched the previous gentleman walk away in tears my heart was heavy, but I also realized The Spirit was getting His message through. One man remained who'd waited intentionally and he asked me to tell his story to everyone I had the opportunity to do so to help reinforce the Love & Lordship message.

He introduced himself and began, "I'm in my late 60s. I was married right out of Bible College, trained in preaching, a full-time seminarian, full-time bi-vocational pastor and within a few short years we had two boys. After hearing your message on God's Covenant order, priority of relationships, and relational servant-leadership, I just had to share my story," he said with a lump in his throat and tears in his eyes.

He asked me, "What do you think got left out?" I replied, "Your marriage and your wife." He told me that for nearly 20 years he had done what he'd been taught through his family and at Bible College and seminary.

As parents we should be attentive to this and while we certainly can point out and reward accomplishment and performance, we must dig deeper and find the issues of character so we can praise, reward, and help develop that inward compass in our children's lives.

This is a blessing to them as they mature and it is also a tremendous blessing to us as parents to see the self-control and self-discipline so crucial to developing character in our children. This carries over into the peaceful home we all desire.

The world is mesmerized by self-esteem, but in reality that is just another prideful motive that ultimately destroys. The real trophy, or jewel, that our children need is to know their self-worth. Let me give you a simple yet profound equation that I pray will help you in developing this in your children and home:

Self-discipline/self-control ⇨ self-respect ⇨ self-worth ⇨ self-love

Think back over teachings in this book and see how this aligns with the greatest commands in that it takes self-discipline/control to die to self and worship God above all. As we mature in our faith and praise, we grow to love Him with all that we are. This produces the self-respect that comes from knowing and loving who we are in Him, which gives us our self-worth. Now we are able to love others.

Unless we are willing to practice the self-discipline/control that forms the character in our lives, we will never develop the self-respect and self-worth needed to go outside ourselves and love others fully.

Ralph Waldo Emerson wrote, "Happy will that house be in which relations are formed from character." We all desire a home filled with happiness and peace and it is Godly character that makes it a reality. If you would like a great resource that helps identify the character traits of God, I highly recommend Character First as they have done an incredible job of studying to identify God's traits that flow from His Truth and love found in Scripture.

Check out this brief chart to give you an idea so you can recognize and be a parent that looks for and praises character as much and more than accomplishment and performance. Here are just a few of the traits from Character First.

Accomplishment is the results we can see; character is what gets you there:

Praise – Two kinds

1) For <u>Accomplishment</u>
   - Good grades
   - Touchdowns
   - Chores

2) For <u>Character</u>
   - Patience
   - Responsibility
   - Initiative
   - Self-Control

5) Never punish in anger or from pride–be sure to check your own motives and selfishness whenever applying punishment with your children–very difficult in tense and embarrassing moments, but punishment must be applied in Love.

6) Punishment and reward – Punishment fits the crime; give opportunities to reward for good behavior and heart as well as for good response to punishment (train the heart). Be sure to connect both punishment and reward with character rather than just accomplishment or performance.

7) Involve your children – allow them to help establish foundations and guidelines based on God's Word as you craft and communicate discipline and punishment. Allow them to define their own punishment to the extent they understand the heart issues and can apply it justly. You keep the final say!

God is very straightforward in His Word that His punishment (the literal word in Greek is mastigoō in Hebrews 12:6 is translated as "to scourge" or "to whip") comes to everyone He receives as His child. Why? Because He loves to punish us? Absolutely not, as that makes no sense based on the rest of the story that Christ gave us culminating in The Cross. He then states in verse 8 that if we do not receive the correction, implying punishment, then we are actually not His children.

This is certainly not to advocate child abuse of any kind, but it is to help us understand that punishment is part of God's love and He knows that we will need it as sinful people in a fallen world. I say often, "God is willing to place the 1,000 volt fence before the 1,000 foot cliff. The shock may hurt but you have the chance to learn from it rather than walk off the cliff."

As Ami and I were raising our children our prayer and desire was for them to know all of God's love, knowing that every bit of it, even the tough and sometimes painful part, was for their good. Knowing that as His child, they would at some point receive His punishment out of His love, and instead of them running from it and rebelling against Him we wanted them to see His love and run toward Him.

As they have faced their own consequences and His loving, yet tough, punishment we have seen that prayer come to pass and are so excited about how He has drawn them to Him and grown them in Him!

"Best Decisions I've Made as a Father"

I shared the story in the previous section about being contacted twice and offered the position of national spokesperson for a rising nonprofit. My decision to turn that position down for the sake of my marriage and family flowed from the priorities that The Lord had revealed in my life for placing my marriage and family above myself and all else except for The Lord Himself.

Here are other decisions that I've made that I hope will encourage you as parents as you strive to train your children up in The Lord:

1) **Loving Christ as Lord and pointing my children to their Heavenly Father.**
   This is not just claiming His free gift of salvation and showing up at church from time to time or even on a regular basis. This is making Him the first priority and thought in every choice I've made in my life and spending time in His Word and prayer EVERY day for the past 33+ years. He is the Source if we will avail ourselves of Him, and He must be FIRST (Luke 14:25-35) and as He is so prioritized our children have a much greater chance of knowing Him.

2) **My children know they are third, and are blessed for it.**
   My children know that Christ is first and my wife, their mom, and our marriage is the second highest priority in my life. They have benefited greatly from seeing this lived out, not always perfectly but always striving for it. I know because I've heard them share this openly with their friends when they've seen chaos in other relationships and homes.

3) **Limiting time away from home.**
   Recall the previous story about the two opportunities to be a national spokesperson. Each time my decision was prompted by my love (commitment) for my Lord, my wife, and family above all else.

4) **Saying "No" to other great opportunities.**
   Turning down coaching positions with several high schools and universities as well as coaching and playing opportunities overseas and here in the US because it wasn't best for my family and children.

5) **Choosing to schedule all of my life.**
   I don't just put "work" or social events on my calendar; I put time with my wife and children on my calendar and mark them as priorities. I rarely miss them, as there has been very few "emergencies" that take priority over them.

6) **Being their mentor, literally their coach and discipler.**
   Every dad has the opportunity to do this in one or more areas of their children's lives. It doesn't matter to them if you've coached before or are even very good at it. Most of our children will never make a living from sports or entertainment, etc. But they will make a life from the things they learn from us. Coaching them is an invaluable opportunity to pass on great life lessons and instill the character of Christ.

If you know anything about my dad, you know he practices what he preaches. I am 23 years old, and in my entire life all my memories of my parents have been unwaveringly consistent with God's Word. This has been true in their marriage, their roles as husband and father, wife and mother, and in their parenting.

In their marriage, I have seen my father lead as Christ leads His Bride, the Church. He has exhibited Christ-like faithfulness, firmness, and love to my mom day after day, year after year. As with every relationship, they did not always agree, but my dad was gracious enough to hear my mom out, listen to her wisdom, and come to an agreement with truth and love. My mother has been a constant companion to my dad, lovingly and willfully submitting to his leadership and servanthood. She was always comfortable voicing her opinion when she disagreed, and knew she was heard and loved unconditionally. She reciprocated that love every day, without fail. Despite the hard times, whether financially, spiritually, or relationally, they have stood by one another as best friends and godly lovers. As a son, I always knew I had amazing examples of parents and a godly marriage.

In their parenting, my mom and dad were partners. They were a team, working together to raise my siblings and me to the best of their ability and trusting God to fill in the gaps where they fall short. When we messed up, they always gave us "punishment that fit the crime," and always out of love and truth. As I've grown into a young man, I wouldn't trade anything to have any other parents in my life. I was always sure that my parents loved me and wanted what was best for me, an excellent example of God's love to His children.

My parents are by no means perfect. They made mistakes, as every human being does. However, I had a daily example of what it means to be a good husband, father, and godly man in my dad. I knew what kind of wife and mother I wanted to love because I had an amazing example in my mom. They have faithfully lived out love and lordship in their 29 years of marriage, and I know they will continue to do so until death do they part.

— Harrison Williams

Something that I've always admired about my dad was his ability to selflessly love my mom. This trait has been important to me for a long time, because as I've grown up and been able to see myself become more and more like my mom, it's characteristics like these that I know I can't compromise on when it comes to finding my husband. Ever since I was old enough to understand, and now being almost 21 years old, I've seen several qualities within my parents' marriage that I knew I needed to experience within my own, whenever that day comes.

*"I have disposed of all
my property to my family.
There is one thing more I wish
I could give to them, and that
is the Christian religion.
If they had that and I had not
given them one cent, they would
be rich. If they have not that,
and I had given them the world,
they would be poor"*

— Patrick Henry

Key Questions

1) What is God's design for marriage, family, and Christ's Church?
2) What is the first priority of parents with their children?
3) What is the role of parents regarding Authority with and for our children?
4) What is the role of parenting in discipline, loving punishment, and discipleship?
5) How do we show love in both discipline and punishment?
6) What are the 3 D's that indicate a need for loving punishment?

Discussions

1) How can you show God's Love and Authority in your parenting?
2) How can you train for character rather than just behavior change?
3) Discuss the connection of love, authority, discipleship, discipline, and punishment.
4) What does the Character of Christ look like in us as we parent our children (what does it mean to be men and women of The Word)?
5) How are you praising and encouraging—loving—your children? What legacy is it leading to?

"Strength of character may be acquired at work, but beauty of character is learned at home. There the affections are trained. There the gentle life reaches us, the true heaven life. In one word, the family circle is the supreme conductor of Christianity."

— Henry Drummond

"It is a trustworthy statement: if any man aspires to the office of elder (or overseer), it is a fine work he desires **to do... He must be** one who manages his own household well, keeping his children under control with all dignity (but if a man does not know how to manage his own household, how will he take care of the church of God?)." (1 Timothy 3:1, 4-5) (NASB, emphasis in original text)

In God's Covenant design, how are we to build the loving fellowship of believers called out as His Church except that we first, just as He did, begin with the loving relationships of marriage and family? This is where both love and leadership are trained and matured in God's design and according to His Word. When we miss it here the church is crippled. Today's church is crippled!

is where we learn to love, lead and disciple, and the Church benefits from focusing on and helping husbands and wives, mothers and fathers, to do so. Not just attend church and youth group and related activities.

Two Stories of Modern-day Home & Church Leadership

Much of the culture of the modern-day Western church has opted for a corporate success model based on marketing principles and attraction rather than a Kingdom fruit model based on disciples maturing and making disciples as branches in The Vine (John 15:1-8). The currency of Christ's Kingdom is loving relationships and the fruit is disciples making disciples, not just in numbers but in obedience and accountability to His Word and Spirit. This is the only way we learn to love and lead according to God's Word.

A Leader in Business & Church...but not at Home

A dear friend and supporter of my ministry to this day came up to me after a men's speaking engagement over 15 years ago where I addressed priorities of relationships with regard to marriage, family, and the church. He was a very successful businessman and a long-time elder in a large and influential church.

He began by saying, "Don't do what I've done. Be sure you keep your priorities in the right place as you've shared with us."

He then told how his wife came to him at Christmas one year and asked him how many Sundays he'd been home the past year?

He frustratingly answered, "I don't know, 25 or so," assuming in his answer that Sundays meant "weekends" giving himself more credit than deserved.

She immediately and intuitively picked up on it (as most wives do) and said, "I'm talking about just Sundays as you weren't home one single full weekend."

He replied curtly, "Yes, I was."

She retorted, "How many Sundays this entire year?"

Now he was angry and said, "At least half of them."

She said, "Do you really want to know how many Sundays you've been home with your family this last year?"

"Sure," he quipped.

"You've been home three Sundays the entire year and not one single full weekend or Saturday."

He angrily denied it. She went and got the calendar and showed him proof of her statement. She then said, "Your daughter is 11 years old and you've missed her growing up. Your son is now 3. Are you going to miss him growing up as well?"

He told me this got his attention and he immediately began to change

He knew she was serious so he immediately called to the senior minister's office. "My wife just gave me an ultimatum: marriage or ministry?"

The senior minister said, "We've been trying to tell you this for eight years."

To which I thought, "Shame on you, senior minister, as you were in a position to turn off his office lights and be sure that he spent more time at home rather than continue to 'build the church' to the detriment of his marriage and family."

The senior minister wisely told him to get to his quiet place with The Lord, pray, and get this worked out. There would be no youth activities this weekend. They both would call his wife and confirm the plan.

He called and then got in his car and spent the next 10 minutes driving to his quiet place while "praying"—he actually said he was defending his work for The Lord—questioning why this was happening. When he arrived he spent five more minutes "praying," and then there was a clear interruption in his thoughts. It wasn't audible, but he knew it was The Lord.

"Son, why are you having an affair with My Bride? I can use you to help with her if you will take care of your bride first."

He said it hit him like a ton of bricks and he knew it was not only The Holy Spirit, but it was also in line with God's Word.

He immediately left in tears and hurried home to his wife to apologize and ask for her forgiveness. She was skeptical as she'd heard similar things before, but this was different so she accepted his apology and forgave him.

Together they moved out of church ministry and began ministering to marriages and families. In recent years they have planted a church in Russia based on discipleship in marriage and family ministry.

churches he had planted that is just as relevant and applicable to our churches today if we will heed the Word of The Holy Spirit.

"It is a trustworthy statement: if any man aspires to the office of overseer, it is a fine work he desires to do. An overseer, then, must be above reproach, the husband of one wife, temperate, prudent, respectable, hospitable, able to teach, not addicted to wine or pugnacious, but gentle, peaceable, free from the love of money. **He must be one who manages his own household well, keeping his children under control with all dignity (but if a man does not know how to manage his own household, how will he take care of the church of God?)**, and not a new convert, so that he will not become conceited and fall into the condemnation incurred by the devil. And he must have a good reputation with those outside the church, so that he will not fall into reproach and the snare of the devil." (1 Timothy 3:1-7 NASB) (Bold mine and added)

The word overseer (*episkopos* in Greek) equates to guardian or pastor. In Paul's letter to Titus (1:5) the word used translates as elder, pointing to the same thing, denoting a high position of leadership in the church. He continues in the same chapter with similar qualifications for servant-leaders called deacons. And what are the outlined qualifications for these extremely important positions to lead Christ's Church?

There are six general qualifications outlined in these verses with much of it centered around marriage and family:

1) He should necessarily be an older person as the Greek word for elder, presbyteros, (Titus 1:5) literally means an older person or advanced in years or life (v. 2 – overseer or bishop). With first century life expectancies likely shorter than ours today as well as younger marrying ages, we are better off to apply the principle as to a stage of life rather than a specific age based on the other requirements listed below, in particular that of maturity in the faith and servant-leading our families. In other words, an elder may have fully grown and married children and even had grandchildren by their late 30s or early 40s. That stage today would likely be 10 – 12 years later.

2) Ability to teach and lead or shepherd – ability to teach is specifically mentioned and scholars agree that a key role and definition of an overseer, pastor, or elder is shepherding – (v. 2).

3) Personal maturity and behavior – must be mature and disciplined, above reproach, in his own behavior personally, relationally, financially, and spiritually, including the husband of one wife (vv. 2-3).

4) Mature in the faith – strong in his faith and not a young believer so he is not prone to pride and easily lured away by the flesh and the world (v. 6).

One of the lead pastors asked me if I would come and teach this to the current elders in the church. I said, "Let me know." I'm still waiting.

The very next year I had three elders approach me and asked if they could nominate me for the position of elder. I gave the same answer. They rebutted with the same questions as the pastors and I replied with the same response. Two of the three had very little communication with me after that exchange.

I can only surmise as to the reason for that and chose not to do so for their sake and mine. However, as stated earlier, I can tell you that it is prominent in our churches that the one qualification that is, shall we say, watered down or ignored is the one that The Holy Spirit prompted Paul to ask: "If a man does not know how to manage or relationally servant-lead, according to God's Word on authority and leadership, in his own family then how can he manage Christ's Family or Church?"

This doesn't just mean to get married and produce offspring. In line with the rest of the teaching of Scripture as described in this book, it means we must invest the time, effort, and teaching to train our children to become the Godly young men and women that He desires them to be and entrusted us to make it happen.

Deception & Its Fruit

We must be honest with ourselves and with others if we are going to apply God's Word to our lives, homes, and to Christ's Church. Otherwise we will continue to prioritize cultural success above Kingdom fruit!

> **We have mastered the art of loving and leading "from afar" in community and systems, such as corporate or governing relationships (including the church), all the while neglecting to be obedient to God's Word to love and lead first in the most intimate of relationships—marriage and family!**

C.S. Lewis said it this way, writing to his nephew and understudy, veteran tempter Screwtape reveals a little secret about human beings: we are incurably idealistic. "Do what you will," he warns, "there is going to be some benevolence, as well as some malice, in your patient's soul. The great thing is to direct the malice to his immediate neighbours whom he meets every day and thrust his benevolence out to the remote circumference, to people he does not know. The malice thus becomes wholly real and the benevolence largely imaginary." —C.S. Lewis, ***The Screwtape Letters***

Here are several issues to consider as we determine whether and where we are compromising on God's Word and in His Church:

1) PRIDE – It looks a lot better to be on a church board than to do the humble work of raising and training our children as a prerequisite to leading His Church. We must humble ourselves and seek His Word and will above our own positions of influence or recognition. This is always subtle but prevalent when held up against the standard and teaching that marriage and family must be the precursor to relational servant-leadership in His Church.

2) There is a lack of truth teaching on relationships, sexuality, marriage, and family and relational servant-leadership – much of the modern day church speak of servant-leadership but ignore or are passé when it comes to God's command to practice and master it first in the home. When we fail to teach and hold accountable for obedience to His word on relationships, sexuality and marriage, we not only see the destruction in our families—we see the fallout in relationships and leadership in our churches.

3) Marriage/Family is devalued by culture and not truthfully defended by our churches as defined in Scripture – compromise, soft-selling, or silence on the issues of relationships, sexuality, and marriage gives our young people, and now even middle age and older, the illusion that the world's values on these issues is perfectly fine as long as

to call and help others do the same, to die to self so we can truly live for Him?

I ask these questions with nearly every man, every couple, and at every event, to spotlight God's teaching on true love and relational servant-leadership according to His design and commands:

1) Do you desire to lead in God's Kingdom? To which many answer, "Yes."
2) From where will He draw and designate His Kingdom leaders? To which a few will answer, "From His Church."
3) From where does His Word say the leaders in His Church are to come? To which very few will answer, "The marriage and family, the home?" (Often done so as a question rather than an answer).
4) Are you preparing yourself to be a leader in His Church, according to His Word, in your marriage and family? To which few answer at all.

We must be careful in identifying and selecting relational servant-leaders in Christ's Church. They will only be able to take us as far as they've gone. Too many today have gone far in leading the world but not their family and yet we call them to lead our churches in contradiction to God's Word. In 1 Timothy 3:4-5, The Holy Spirit, through Paul, poses the poignant question, "How can you lead my family if you can't or aren't servant-leading yours?"

Remember from earlier chapters that Christ is The Author and true authority comes from Him. Relational servant-leadership is His concept and model of authority. We have far too often opted for the culture's pseudo-leadership and brought it into our churches. We must repent and change so we are training the leaders in our homes and then in His Church that will truly impact the world for His Kingdom and Glory!

Scriptural Solutions

How are we to do this? I'm going to briefly propose the answers that lie in Scripture for training disciples, building Christ-like character and healthy relationships that honor marriage and family, and reflect His Truth and loving image. We could do entire studies and books on each of these but I'm just including the principles and related Scriptures for your personal study and growth as His disciple.

Here are seven Scriptural solutions that take us right back through the principles of His Love and Lordship in this book. We can and are called to do this as we trust and walk in Him and His Truth (most of these principles and texts are a recap of what has been discussed throughout this book):

3) Obedience-based discipleship and maturity in Christ will be the priority and evident in Church teaching and in our relationships and service, beginning in the home and family.
4) We will begin to revalue and rebuild a Kingdom marriage and family culture that emphasizes:
   - Teaching and accountability regarding agape relationships and purity in sexuality;
   - Relational servant-leadership modeled and taught in the home;
   - Generational discipleship beginning in the home and reinforced in churches.
5) Building relationships is taught as part of Spiritual Disciplines and Discipleship rather than deferring to the culture's concept of relationships occurring naturally:
   - Discipling/Mentoring, Serving/Servant-leadership flows from applying Scriptures with the understanding that good relationships are formed in the discipline of The Holy Spirit and in line with God's Word rather than just according to our natural, selfish flesh and desires.
6) Our maturity in Christ focuses on and builds a family-based Body or Church rather than a corporate and business-based model driven by goals and outcomes.
7) The Biblical emphasis of discipleship and loving relationships as Kingdom fruit takes priority and drives decision-making with regard to growth, finances, service, programs and all other elements rather than the reverse.
8) A familial and relational Church develops disciples who serve, give, share, and lead as a result of priority principles of Christ's Lordship and our discipleship rather than service opportunities and programs masquerading as discipleship. Service is essential in discipleship and Church growth but, for the most part, should flow from study and maturity, personally and relationally, and the expectation of, and growth in, obedience rather than preceding it.

here implies that they would need to voraciously partake of this Bread or they would have no life in them). In other words, they must believe in Him with all their heart or there was no eternal life for them (vv. 51, 53). When He finished many disciples knew it was a very difficult thing He was asking so they walked away and no longer followed Him (v. 66).

I asked the minister if he thought that was a fair answer to his question and even more importantly was it a Biblical response? He nodded his head in agreement, and then with head bowed and shoulders slumped, he walked away.

The Whole Truth

I wholeheartedly believe that most pastors, small or large church, desire for people to know Jesus as Savior and Lord. I also believe that many have gotten caught up in attracting folks (miracles and healings from previous story that translates in various ways to how to keep them coming) rather than truly making disciples. I pray that whatever the case may be that we take to heart Jesus' words: to place Him above all else; that loving Him is obeying Him; and we begin to prioritize our marriages, families, and homes to obedience-based discipleship that builds His Church and advances His Kingdom. And the gates of Hell will not prevail against it!

In 2005, I read some information about a survey that came to be known as the Reveal Survey at Willow Creek Community Church (WCCC) in the Chicago area. This was one of the fastest growing and largest churches in America and their executive minister had asked their senior minister if they could use some of the budget for a discipleship survey to "gauge the depth" of discipleship in their growth.

Long story short—the survey (you can find it if you just Google the info above) revealed not only that they were not making disciples, but those who were more mature in their faith were stagnating. In addition, those in the largest two groups—seekers and new believers—showed very little, if any, growth when they should have shown the most and the most rapid maturation.

Before the results were published and spoken about, WCCC asked 30 of their own church plants across the country to take the survey. It resulted in statistically the same results. Here's what they found (these are my words but generally capture the findings):

1) There were four groups of people in their church with the largest being "seekers" and "new/young believers." The other two groups were those "maturing in Christ" and "mature in Christ."

2) There was very little movement except that growth continued in the first two groups by numbers but not in maturity of their faith.

This is Christ's command and He has given us all we need to be His disciples and make disciples as we trust in Him and are obedient to His Word.

Only then are we really taking His message to a world that needs it. They will probably not like it initially; but those who have eyes to see and ears to hear the difference cannot help but answer clearly one way or another that they desire to be His or want no part of Him. Let's make His Love and Lordship clear so they can know.

There has to be a clear difference in our message about Christ and the culture. Ronald Reagan said, *"I've often wondered what Jesus' "Sermon on the Mount" would have looked like if He would have had to run it through most modern-day church boards."*

> *"If a church offers no truth that is not available in the general culture...there is not much reason to pay it attention."*
>
> — Richard John Neuhaus

Key Questions

1) What has been your experience with leadership in your church(es)?
2) Where have you seen good models of servant-leadership in families?
3) Where have you seen good models of servant-leadership in The Church?
4) What do you need to do to lead in your home and/or in His Church according to His Word?
5) How would relational servant-leadership change the way your church's leadership might be structured?

Discussion

1) What is God calling you to do in your family to love and lead more like Christ?
2) Are you preparing yourself in your home to be a servant-leader in Christ's Church?
3) What is the relationship between love, lordship, and servant-leadership?
4) What are you modeling for your children when it comes to love and leading?

"This is a day when practical work is overemphasized, and the saints who are bringing every project into captivity are criticized and told that they are not in earnest for God or for souls. True earnestness is found in obeying God, not in the inclination to serve Him that is born of undisciplined human nature. It is inconceivable, but true nevertheless, that saints are not bringing every project into captivity, but are doing work for God at the instigation of their own human nature which has not been spiritualized by determined discipline.

We are apt to forget that a man is not only committed to Jesus Christ for salvation; he is committed to Jesus Christ's view of God, of the world, of sin and of the devil, and this will mean that he must recognize the responsibility of being transformed by the renewing of his mind."

— Oswald Chambers, **My Utmost for His Highest**

"'The body is not only biological. The body, as John Paul II unfolds in great detail, is also theological. It tells an astounding divine story. And it does so precisely through the mystery of sexual difference and the call of the two to become 'one flesh.' This means that sex is not just about sex. The way we understand and express our sexuality points to our deepest-held convictions about who we are, who God is, the meaning of love, the ordering of society, and, ultimately, the mystery of the universe. Hence, John Paul II's Theology of the Body (TOB) is much more than a reflection on sex and married love. Through that, it leads us to 'the rediscovery of the meaning of the whole of existence...the meaning of life.'" (TOB 46:6)

"Christ teaches that the meaning of life is found by loving as he loves (see John 15:12). One of John Paul II's main insights is that God inscribed this vocation to love as he loves right in our bodies by creating us male and female and calling us to become 'one flesh' (see Genesis 2:24). Far from being a footnote in the Christian life, the way we understand the body and the sexual relationships 'concerns the whole Bible' (TOB 69:8). It plunges us into 'the perspective of the whole gospel, or the whole teaching even more, of the whole mission of Christ.'" (TOB 49:3)

"Christ's mission is to restore the order of love in a world seriously distorted by sin. And the union of the sexes, as always, lies at the basis of the human 'order of love.' Therefore, what we learn in John Paul II's TOB is obviously 'important with regard to marriage.' However it is equally essential and valid for the (understanding) of man in general: for the fundamental problem of understanding him and for the self-understanding of his being in the world." (TOB 102:5)

— Christopher West, **Theology of the Body**

themselves we have forced other cultures and countries to comply through financial incentives or held them hostage with financial restrictions, such as withholding government funding for HIV-AIDS or other program funding if they will not agree to teach and promote the condom and contraception based sex education.

When we comply, by consent or silence, we are allowing the enemy to attack the very foundations of God's creation and order from the beginning.

The reason I'm focusing on this area as we discuss how to take this message to a lost and hurting world is because this is the core issue and the greatest ammunition the enemy has in destroying the foundations that God laid down at creation. In His design, male and female were created for marriage in a lifetime monogamous covenant commitment and sex is reserved for this union only. When porn is disguised as "education" and deceitfully marketed as "safe," it goes directly against all that is God and His Truth and Love.

As stated earlier in this book, porn/porneia is the greatest destroyer of love and relationship and the only thing that will overcome it is the power of the Gospel lived out through His families and Church.

If we are going to re-establish the foundations of God's Word in marriage, family, and His Church then we must expose and stand firm against this evil. We must be as wise as serpents and as cunning as doves. And we must not be afraid to proclaim His whole Truth regarding relationships, marriage, family and sexuality.

Exporting Porn & "Churchianity"

In 1991, just after Ami and I were married, I was asked to sit in with a few other folks at the church where we were members and interact with Pastor Shu of the underground church in China. After four hours of listening to him and his interpreter, we were each given the opportunity to ask one question. Needless to say, he'd heard them all.

Being the last to ask, I pulled the reporter's trick and combined two questions into one, "How can we help and what can we learn from you?"

Pastor Shu had spent no more than one minute on the other questions and did the same with the first of mine, "We don't need you to teach us how to do church. We need money and Bibles." He then proceeded to elaborate for nearly 30 more minutes in answering the second question and tying it into the first.

He said, "The American Church needs to learn humility. You look at the buildings and numbers, your missionary outreach, and count those as success and think The Lord is blessing you. Well, He has, but God is taking His hands off the American Church." You could hear a pin drop.

He continued to explain, "For the first 20 or so years (mid-60s to mid-80s) when our young men wanted to enter into the ministry/pastorate, we

Why have we, as Christ's Church, allowed the world to dictate when and where His Truth can be spoken and applied? It is the only thing that will set people free, but we claim graciousness in withholding His Word in politics, schools, media, and more while Satan continues to enslave.

Here are some current issues and outcomes that give evidence to our fear and timidity, and Paul said: "For God has not given us a spirit of timidity, but of power and love and discipline." (1 Timothy 1:7 NASB)

CURRENT OUTCOMES/POTENTIAL STRUGGLES
Present & Eternal

- Emotionally-driven salvation
- Very lacking in obedience-based discipleship
- Spiritually immature, fleshly driven service
- Focus on people above God
- Churches and Christians that look and act like the culture – Conformed to the world

All of these have been addressed throughout this book as a response to Jesus' own prophecy of Judgment Day in Matthew 7:21-23: "Not everyone who says to Me, 'Lord, Lord,' will enter the kingdom of heaven, but he who does the will of My Father who is in heaven will enter. Many will say to Me on that day, 'Lord, Lord, did we not prophesy in Your name, and in Your name cast out demons, and in Your name perform many miracles?' And then I will declare to them, 'I never knew you; DEPART FROM ME, YOU WHO PRACTICE LAWLESSNESS.'"

The only thing that we have any control over in this prophecy is whether we are contributing to the "many" whom Jesus refers to or working to diminish the "many" that don't really know Him and add to the souls that do!

> *"When the foundations are destroyed, what can the righteous do?"*
>
> *— Psalm 11:3*

It's obvious, or should be, as to the current dilemma. How do we as Christ's people address and confront the lies and deceptions without compromising His Truth or grace? What is the church currently doing? What do we need to do?

While there are many problems facing our churches today, the focus will be on the issue of porneia or sexual immorality. This permeates our culture and directly attacks the foundations for marriage, family and loving relationships upon which God created the world and that symbolically

In the image above, the blackened leaves and fruit coming from the roots and teachings represent promiscuity, porn, depression, cohabitation, abortion, STDs, teen/unwed pregnancies, divorce, broken homes, and much more, all a direct affront and attack on God's foundations and order.

We learned earlier in this book that in Proverbs 22:6 the Hebrew word for "train up" means to "bend or shape" and it applies to whoever is doing the "discipling or teaching." Those who are sowing the "seeds of destruction" here in US are "discipling" with this message internationally through USAIDS dollars and condom-promotion, free sex agenda. BEWARE!

Again, I ask the question, "Who's discipling our youth?" Let's BE STRONG in standing in God's Truth and sharing His Word to remind others that God alone can take what's wrong and make it right. (Joel 2:25)

"Do I believe that God can deal with my 'yesterday,' and make it as though It had never been? I either do not believe he can, or I do not want Him to. Forgiveness, which is so easy for us to accept, cost God the agony of Calvary. When Jesus Christ says, 'Sin no more,' He conveys the power that enables a man not to sin any more, and that power comes by right of what He did on the Cross." Oswald Chambers, *Still Higher for His Highest*

Current Church Paradigm: Symptomatic Response – Conformed to the World/Reaping What Is Sown

Romans 12:2 states that we are not to conform to the world and Galatians 6:7-8 remind us that the outcome of doing so is that we will reap what we sow.

There have been some attempts in today's churches, but for the most part they have followed the knowledge-based teaching and a symptomatic response with little positive impact. The following graphic is what the efforts and fruit look like as the modern church has implemented its strategies and programs.

"Make a tree good and its fruit will be good, or make a tree bad and its fruit will be bad, for a tree is recognized by its fruit." (Matthew 12:33)

Churches enter with a symptomatic response of some great programs – marriage prep, enrichment, mentoring, reconciliation, divorce recovery, possibly Sexual Risk Avoidance programs that teach and encourage abstinence and building healthy relationships. This results in some saved marriages and restored families, which is wonderful, but far too many are still exposed to the filth and immorality of the "free sex" programs and reap the consequences.

How often have our classes, programs and ministries, again even with the greatest of hearts and intentions, fallen flat because we have either ignored His priorities and order or we have been blinded to them and

Yes, it requires diligence, but it will be worth it as we see marriages, homes, and families that are the building blocks of His Bride and Family, the Church. Then because of the life-infusing examples of marriages and loving, Godly relationships, the world will clamor for this kind of love that they obviously are not seeing presently! This doesn't mean there aren't good examples and some wonderful relationships out there, but the reality is that in our churches and certainly in the larger culture there is a glaring absence of this.

I do not think at all that it's because we don't care. I think it's because, in our desire to see people saved, we've "redesigned" His order to draw people in to hear the Gospel message, which is so important. However, the enemy has taken full advantage of our heartfelt but misplaced priorities when it comes to expecting obedience and building loving relationships. (John 14:15, 21; 1 Peter 1:22; 1 John 2:5; 5:2).

"Does the Lord delight in burnt offerings and sacrifices as much as in obeying the Lord? To obey is better than sacrifice, and to heed is better than the fat of rams. For rebellion is like the sin of divination, and arrogance like the evil of idolatry. Because you have rejected the word of the Lord, He has rejected you as king." (1 Samuel 15:22–23)

There's a better way and it is found in the very essence of this book. Obedience-based discipleship under Christ's teaching in our families with churches stepping up to reinforce the messages and help encourage obedience and accountability with grace and Truth! Strengthen the family and we all win!

Let's show the world what it really means to live in His Love & Lordship!

In order to truly change and deal with the sin in our personal and relational lives and help those who are lost, we must make Him Lord and walk as His disciples!

This ultimately means that we cannot assume that those in the world around us, or even those who sit in our churches, understand His Love and Lordship (Authority). They will likely be living by these false assumptions. It is imperative that we understand His Word, that he reigns in our lives, and our desire is that we share it with others by word and deed. We must not make the mistake of thinking that most of the people we interact with grasp what this means in their lives and relationships.

Look around, folks. Even in many of our churches we've placated based on these wrong assumptions of His Love and Lordship. The evidence is overwhelming. We're not getting it or passing it on as disciples making disciples in our homes, churches, or communities.

This must change! Christ's prophetic warning in Matthew 7:21–23 has everything to do with a right relationship with Him that is then lived out and observed by the world in our relationships, first in our families and then in His Church. We must truly receive by His grace through faith (Ephesians 2:8-9), and then strive to live out this priority relationship with Him (Philippians 2:12-13). This is what gives us His Authority in the lives of others as they will see it and invite us to have influence in their lives—True Authority lived out in Love!

Talk of our civilization or society crumbling over bogus and pseudo rights is not the problem. We will not crumble because these are not being protected, rather we will crumble with the lawless, immoral and unethical continuation of so-called "rights." Every global power that has existed and subsequently "died out" did so from the moral collapse within – and every bit of it was posited as something good, right or moral - actually to mask the indulgent, selfish and pleasurable! How stubborn or downright blind do we need to be to see that the exact same immoralities posed as moral, right and good are what is deteriorating our culture and society today? It is happening (and is evident) in every part of our culture – government, media, education, religion (church) and home/family! Who will stand for the Truth about right, good and morality? That is who will either make a difference or be persecuted for trying and in the end will be proven right!

God's Covenant Design

Why is this important? We must remember that God's design from the beginning moves from the individual to the relational (marriage and family) into the community (Church) and finally into any systems (governments and nations).

STUDY GUIDE
WISE AS SERPENTS, GENTLE AS DOVES

Key Concepts

1) We must be prepared as Christ's disciples to take His message to the world.
2) Preparation calls for us to be studied, obedient, wise and gracious.
3) Modern day outcomes include emotionally based "salvation," a lack of obedience-based discipleship, spiritual immaturity and fleshly driven service.
4) Cultural Christianity places emphasis on people above God.
5) Restoring the foundations of Lordship, discipleship, Godly marriage, families, and relationships is essential to reviving The Church.
6) The greatest destroyer of loving relationships is sexual immorality or porneia.
7) The culture spreads the "safe sex" message of porneia as perfectly fine and disguised as "education."
8) The fruit of the sexual revolution in our families, churches and culture is immorality and destruction as we are reaping what we have sown.
9) The churches' response is predominantly symptomatic.
10) The Church needs to respond with the foundational principles of relational integrity and sexual purity within marriages and families, with churches and families then supporting each other in obedience-based discipleship.
11) God's order is to move from the individual to relationships to community to corporate or systemic. If we do not heed His Word with individuals and in relationships, we will not be able to curtail it in our communities or systems.
12) The Scriptural paradigm of the Love and Lordship message is: Lordship⇨Discipleship⇨Relationships⇨Sin/Issues/Problems.

MARRIAGE/FAMILY MINISTRIES & RESOURCES

WEBSITES
Grace Marriage: www.gracemarriage.com
Marriage Savers: www.marriagesavers.org
FamilyLife: www.familylife.com
All Pro Dad: www.allprodad.com
American Family Association: afa.net
Focus on the Family: www.focusonthefamily.com
Homeword: www.homeword.com
Pure Life Ministries: www.purelifeministries.org
Faithful and True: www.faithfulandtrue.com
L.I.F.E. Ministries International: www.freedomeveryday.org
Marriage Today: www.marriagetoday.com
MERCY: www.mercyky.org

MOVIES
Fireproof: www.kendrickbrotherscatalogue.com/fireproof
Courageous: www.kendrickbrotherscatalogue.com/courageous
War Room: www.kendrickbrotherscatalogue.com/warroom/home
Overcomer: www.kendrickbrotherscatalogue.com/overcomer
Like Arrows: www.familylife.com/likearrows

BOOKS
Love and Respect by Emerson Eggerichs
Uncompromised Faith by S. Michael Craven
Kingdom Man and Kingdom Marriage by Dr. Tony Evans
His Needs, Her Needs by Willard Harley
His Needs, Her Needs for Parents by Willard Harley
Sacred Marriage by Gary Thomas
Sacred Parenting by Gary Thomas
Cherish by Gary Thomas
The Five Love Languages by Gary Chapman
Parenting by the Book by John Rosemond
What He Must Be...if he wants to marry my daughter by Dr. Voddie Baucham
A Chicken's Guide to Talking Turkey with Your Kids About Sex by Dr. Kevin Leman
Questions Kids Ask About Sex edited by Melissa Cox

"The Love & Lordship message is a wake-up call to the married and engaged within Christ's body– the Church–to emulate, pursue, and reflect His purpose and design for marriage. Pursuing pure love, grace, hope, truth, integrity, and intimacy with Christ and with one's spouse or future spouse are essential in a strong Christ-centered marriage. Our generation must heed the LORD's warning: "Unless the LORD builds the house, the builders labor in vain" Psalm 127:1. This message focuses on the importance of being one-in-Christ as a married couple. A timely equipping to fight against the culture of divorce within the Church."

— Terry Sikes, Sr. Pastor, Joshua, TX

"Greg Williams led me and my wife through the Love & Lordship message when our lives were spiraling out of control. His wisdom and guidance led by The Holy Spirit helped save our marriage.

We acknowledge the Biblical truth that Greg spoke into our marriage helped us to overcome our unfaithfulness to each other and to God. When the world told us to divorce, Greg told us to repent and save our commitment that we made to each other many years ago. Since then, we have been blessed with 10 years of a renewed life, a redeemed marriage and two beautiful kids. Greg helped us turn our mess into our message. As we reflect, we are eternally thankful that God led us to Greg during our adversity."

— Clif and Stacey Marshall, Bloomington, IN

"God's message through your Love & Lordship class helped me more than anything I've ever heard to get out of addiction and get my life back."

— Paul Smith, Isaiah House staff and former resident

"That was the most "nutritious" Christ-centered presentation I have heard in years; thought-provoking and presented with passion!"

— Doug Seminick, Louisville, KY

"The Lord is using Greg and the
Love & Lordship Ministry in tremendous ways!
My wife and I first met Greg at the Love and Lordship conference which was hosted by our church, Calvary Christian of Winchester, KY. The two-day seminar was powerful! Never have I met someone with such passion and enthusiasm for healthy marriages and families. He's a hard-hitter, sometimes the content is tough, challenging and convicting but I can truthfully say that Greg used the Word of God to breathe new life into my marriage.

Our church body was so blessed by the Love and Lordship conference that we didn't think twice about bringing Greg back as the keynote speaker for the 2018 Calvary Christian Men's Retreat– Bluegrass Christian Camp.

Love & Lordship and my Brother in Christ, Greg, have had an incredibly positive impact in my family's life. It is truly our honor and privilege to support their ministry and we are excited to see where the Lord will take them in 2019!"

— Chris and Amanda Tucker, Winchester, KY

"Love & Lordship has taught me the importance of living my marriage centered in Christ. I've learned that being the spiritual leader of my family while serving my wife is pleasing to God and honors Him.

— Jeff Hancock, Lexington, KY

"I heartily recommend Greg Williams and Love & Lordship. Greg's gift of communication coupled with eye opening information regarding our culture is a presentation that should be heard across our nation. The relevant and gripping evidences presented challenge the heart, mind, and moral conscience of anyone who cares about their children and this country. Love & Lordship is about truths that can make a difference."

— Ernie Perry, Sr. Minister,
Indian Creek Christian Church, Cynthiana, KY

"Thank you! This was one of the best conferences we've been to and one of the best messages we've heard!"

— Sean and Beth McCreary, Marriage Mentors,
Ninevah Christian Church, Lawrenceburg, KY

"The traditional American family is under assault and getting weaker by the day. Restoring it to its original purpose and function will only happen by highly intentional effort. Greg Williams provides key instruction and motivation for men to become diligent disciples, humble husbands and faithful fathers. A relevant and powerful message presented in a clear and effective way. Expect to be radically changed from the inside out!"

— Kent Laufenburger, Lexington, KY

"Everyone we've spoken with in the days since this workshop thought it was well worth their time. Many of us think this course should be required material prior to any couple getting married."

— Nita and Butch Pulliam, Prospect, KY

"What a great seminar. I really appreciated the biblical depth of your teaching; it took me back to some of my favorite Bible classes in college. My wife was unfortunately unable to get out of work that night, but I shared my notes with her when we both got home. She and I got married in August and I get the feeling we'll be drawing from your insights for many years to come! I think the people of our church were greatly blessed and challenged from your message. Thanks for the thoughtfulness and passion with which you made it happen."

— Zach Price, Prospect, KY

"Thank you, Greg, for sharing with couples at The Marriage Education and Resource Center (MERCY) from his seminar Love & Lordship. He did a great job and his passion for marriage and family is so evident. Here are a few comments from some of our participants: 'Well done and great info.' 'The greatest of these is love. We learn the truth about this, we learn the ultimate truth.' 'I've heard no greater explanation of agape love.' We so appreciate the work Greg is doing through Love & Lordship."

— David and Penny Hudson, MERCY, Crestwood, KY

"My husband and I attended the Love & Lordship conference this weekend, and I walked away so filled and so overwhelmed with the Holy Spirit. The way God moved through the message was amazing. I loved it. God has been working on me over the past 4 years (married 4 years in November)...my husband's first marriage and my 4th. After this message, I realize it's taken me 40 years and 3 marriages to learn how to love. My husband has fallen away from God and is caring for his elderly mother. This conference couldn't have come at a better time in both of our lives. God is always good and His timing amazing. We both say 'thank you' for bringing God's word in a message so profound and real, and right to the heart. After all these years, I finally get it. This message from God will change lives, families and marriages. Thank you, thank you, thank you for God's message on marriage.Bless you and your ministry."

— Dianne and Calvin Petrey, Lexington, KY

"I took and graduated the Love & Lordship class with Greg and not only is he an amazing teacher, but taught me about my Lord and Savior with such a passion it was unrealistic. Now, knowing and loving Jesus Christ I am able to love the rest of my family. Hats off to you Greg; you are doing an amazing job."

— Jacob Holland, Former REVIVE Lifehouse Resident and Current Staff, Nicholasville, KY

"We first experienced Love & Lordship at our church when Greg Williams came to share a weekend family conference for our congregation. He returned about a year later and shared a deeper dive series in our Sunday School time. We were immediately impacted with the order of priorities in our lives as compared to the biblical view. He shared about the marriage covenant and that changed our marriage. God-Marriage-Spouse was a mind shift for us, and helped us through a difficult time. Love & Lordship is a teaching and discipline that impacts the marriage, parenting, friendships, and overall spiritual life. After over 14 years of marriage, I can say Love and Lordship brought us to a healthy relationship for the first time. God calls it oneness, we call it happiness...and Peace in our house/home."

— Joe and Jennifer Sykes, Paris, KY

"Thank you for sharing the vision that God has given you regarding Love and Lordship–especially how it relates to the family unit that God has entrusted us with. One of the points that impacted us was the realization that anytime we put the church or even our marriage/family above the authority of God, we are in idolatry. Your exposition of Philippians 3:7-11 brought home the point of seeking God and a vibrant relationship with Jesus above all. As marriage mentors, we see couples all the time that are living their life out of balance. Your message reminded and challenged us (both personally as a couple and as partners in marriage ministry) of the importance of keeping the main thing the main thing!

Another point we really appreciated was your focus on servant leadership. The many examples you provided from Matthew 20:24-28 and John 13 were welcome reminders of the importance of serving our spouse, family, and those outside of our home. As you mentioned, real influence is invited influence, which comes from humility and service. This runs parallel with a statement made by Francis Chan in his last marriage book that if our focus is on others and God's purpose, we won't be so focused on fighting amongst ourselves.

What a timely message about the importance of the authority of Christ in our families and our church and the need of sacrifice and service for His kingdom. These reminders will be a key focus for our own marriage and family as well as the couples we are working with. When our personal relationships come under the authority of God and we are seeking His kingdom first, the problems in our marriage, family and church are much easier to deal with AND we will have the Spirit and motivation to love and serve others as well."

— Scott and Renee Swicegood, Marriage Ministry,
Central Church, Georgetown, KY

so inspired and motivated to use and share what we learned! We thoroughly enjoyed your presentation and learned so much. We passed on the main point to our Singles Class the next day at church, i.e. getting the vertical relationship right, so that the horizontal relationships will work. You have a great gift and we are so thankful you are using it for this critical issue of our time–strong and lasting marriages. The moral breakdown that our society faces today is largely due to the epidemic of broken marriages.

— Colonel Steve (USAF Retired) and Mrs. Lorrie Parker,
Porter Memorial Baptist Singles Ministry, Lexington, KY

"Love & Lordship is a thought-provoking, Biblically grounded presentation of the Gospel of Christ as the building of His Kingdom from salvation to sanctification and discipleship! Too often in today's culture the soft-sell message of 'salvation-only' dominates the teaching and leaves many without a full understanding of becoming Christ's disciple and helping others do the same—building His Kingdom in every realm of our lives. It often leaves them in bondage to the sin they are supposed to be set free from. This ministry is an encouragement and challenge to the Church to become Christ's followers in every part of their lives—personal, marriage/home/family, business and workplace, government and community as a whole! You will be challenged, although it will be done with gentleness and respect (I Peter 3:15)."

— Tim Philpot, Judge (Retired), Circuit Family Court, Lexington, KY

"The paradigm model for Love & Lordship of Lordship, Discipleship, Relationship, & Sexuality provides an excellent approach to the One True Answer for the pathologies plaguing families today. The prevailing "ME" culture is crumbling the foundations of our homes as well as all other social orders God Himself designed. Greg unequivocally establishes through the Love & Lordship paradigm the only way we can effectively address the woes that confound our society—and that is to recognize the Lordship of our Creator, God; to follow Him in true Discipleship; to acknowledge and willingly submit to the individual roles He ordained in our relationships; and to honor Him and ourselves by respecting the gift of our sexuality, fulfilled in the sanctified, blessed and life-long union of one man and one woman in marriage.

Greg's ability to speak to the cause of societal pathologies and to present the remedies to address them is a complete, comprehensive, and soundly Scripture-based approach. He speaks with compassion and conviction. He captivates the hearer with the boldness and authority of the Word, and credits the Holy Spirit that guides and blesses his own life and family with the power to mend broken hearts and homes to bring healing. He does not promise an easy path or a quick fix for disobedient mistakes. He does promise forgiveness and comfort through repentance and restoration found in Jesus Christ alone.

There are no reservations in my recommendation of Love & Lordship, nor Greg's conviction and heart for those he seeks to reach in a fallen, lost world."

— Allison Reynolds, Broadhead, KY

For more information
and to have Greg Williams speak
at your church or organization,
contact Love & Lordship at
loveandlordship@gmail.com.

www.loveandlordship.com
On Facebook and Twitter
@LoveandLordship
Also on Apple Podcast, Google Play, YouTube and Vimeo

Special acknowledgments

*Thank you Jeff Hancock for the design work on this book
and Jeff Rogers for the cover and portrait photography.*